When a Brother or Sister Dies

When a Brother or Sister Dies

Looking Back, Moving Forward

CLAIRE BERMAN

PRAEGER

Westport, Connecticut
London

Library of Congress Cataloging-in-Publication Data

Berman, Claire.
When a brother or sister dies : looking back, moving forward / Claire Berman.
p. cm.
Includes bibliographical references and index.
ISBN 978–0–313–35528–8 (alk. paper)
1. Bereavement—Psychological aspects. 2. Brothers and sisters—Death—Psychological aspects. I. Title.
BF575.G7B477 2009
306.9—dc22 2008040401

British Library Cataloguing in Publication Data is available.

Library of Congress Catalog Card Number: 2008040401
ISBN: 978–0–313–35528–8

First published in 2009

Praeger Publishers, 88 Post Road West, Westport, CT 06881
An imprint of Greenwood Publishing Group, Inc.
www.praeger.com

Printed in the United States of America

The paper used in this book complies with the Permanent Paper Standard issued by the National Information Standards Organization (Z39.48–1984).

10 9 8 7 6 5 4 3 2 1

In loving memory of
Samuel Gallant

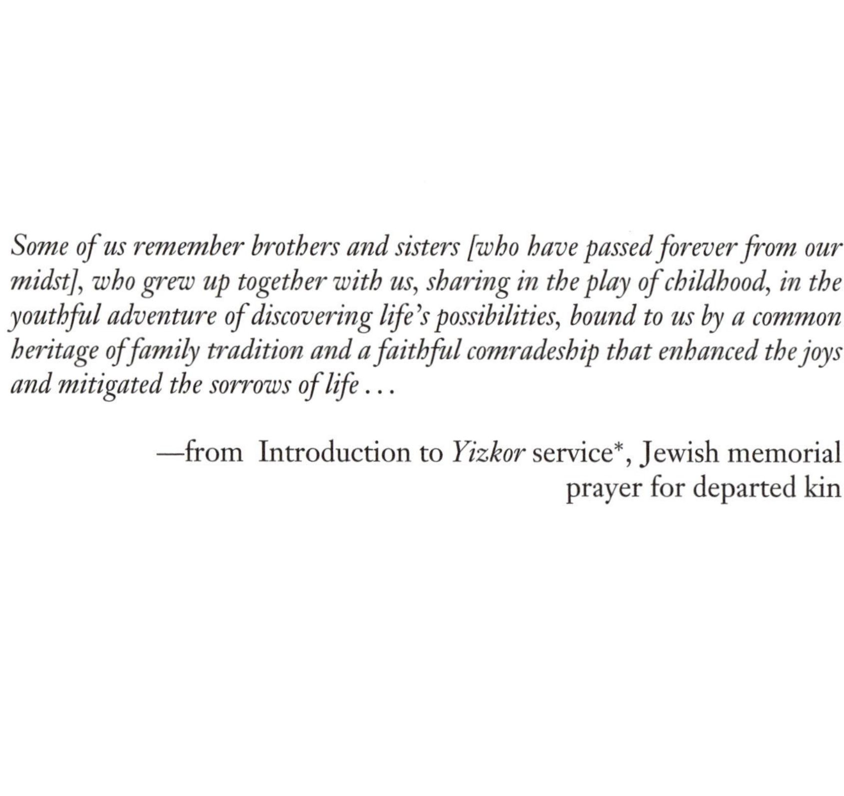

Some of us remember brothers and sisters [who have passed forever from our midst], who grew up together with us, sharing in the play of childhood, in the youthful adventure of discovering life's possibilities, bound to us by a common heritage of family tradition and a faithful comradeship that enhanced the joys and mitigated the sorrows of life . . .

—from Introduction to *Yizkor* service*, Jewish memorial prayer for departed kin

---

*Reprinted by permission of The Jewish Reconstructionist Press [http://www.jrf.org/press]. Call 1-800-JRF-PRESS for publication information.

Contents

Introduction

The week of September 11, 2001, when America lost its innocence, I lost my sister, Sybil, to heart disease.

And my world changed.

I expected that I would outlive Sybil someday, but not this soon. For one thing, she was older than I by almost a decade. For another, she had suffered for years from a variety of ailments. Only one of her kidneys was in good working order; she struggled with diabetes; and she had developed heart disease.

I have before me the image of Sybil in the intensive care unit after she had undergone quadruple bypass surgery: her face pale and bloated like that of a rubberized doll, her body connected by a network of tubes and wires to a mega lineup of machines that burbled and blinked. It was a scene straight out of a science fiction film, disturbing and unforgettable.

Yet Sybil survived, experiencing good periods and bad in the dozen or so years that followed, and was eventually diagnosed with congestive heart failure. In practical terms, this meant that periodically she would grow very weak. Her ankles would swell, her lungs would be surrounded by fluid, and she would have trouble walking, let alone breathing. At those times, she would spend a week or two in a hospital where care would be provided and her medications adjusted. The family referred to these stays as "tune-ups," a routine part of the regimen required to keep Sybil's heart in working order. Following discharge, my sister would return home, resume her job as a teacher, reconnect with her friends. Though sick, she was not sickly. All of us rejoiced each time Sybil rejoined us.

My sister died on September 5, 2001, in the hospital where she had gone for what we all—Sybil included—believed was another tune-up.

My sister died when none of us—doctors, children and grandchildren, family and friends—expected death to take her.

My sister died. But part of me still cannot believe she is gone.

That must be the reason why, years after her death, her name and phone number remain listed on the speed-dial section of my phone. When something good happens, like the birth of a grandchild, the first person I want to call is my sister. When the news is bad, when I am troubled and would like someone to provide words of comfort—more important, just to listen—I want to phone my sister. Returning from a weekend out of town, I feel an urge to check in, and so I touch the button marked "Sybil." But I do not press it down.

My sister died, and I am still trying to understand and deal with it.

I am not alone in the struggle. In America, an estimated 25 percent of people have experienced the death of a brother or sister. One can assume similarly large numbers throughout the world. It is surprising, therefore, that the subject of sibling loss has not received greater attention from specialists in grief and mourning. Instead, we sisters and brothers who live with the loss find that we are forgotten mourners.

A search of the literature underscores the neglect. In his thoughtful and thought-provoking work, *How We Grieve*, for example, Thomas Attig provides many stories of grievers. In one moving tale involving six-year-old Bobby, who kills himself while playing with his father's gun, the philosopher focuses on the grief of the boy's father, mother, and a neighbor child who had witnessed the accident. Bobby's brother and sister, Johnny and Melanie, are mentioned only in passing. *Their* grief is not addressed.

In *Continuing Bonds*, an important work edited by bereavement scholars Dennis Klass, Phyllis Silverman, and Steven Nickman that speaks to the value of maintaining bonds with the deceased following a variety of deaths and losses, we even find discussion of the retroactive loss felt by an adopted person—but *no* chapter on adult sibling bereavement.

Someone recommends that I read *Living with Loss, Healing with Hope*, an inspirational work by Earl Grollman. I find solace and wisdom in the rabbi's words. "Each bereavement is unique," he says, and goes on to explain: the death of a child is the death of one's future; the death of a parent is the death of one's past; the loss of a spouse is the death of the present. The death of a sibling goes unmentioned albeit it is a unique and incalculable loss of past, present, *and* future.

"The sibling relationship is life's longest relationship, longer, for most of us, by a quarter of a century than our ties to our parents," write psychologists Stephen P. Bank and Michael D. Kahn in their groundbreaking study, *The Sibling Bond.* "It is longer than our relationship with our children, certainly longer than with a spouse and, with the exception of a few lucky men and women, longer than with a best friend."

To those of us who are sensitive to the issue, the impact of the death of a sibling is everywhere evident.

In the sports pages of the daily newspaper, we read the tragic account of a ball player who crashed his car into a moving train. Somewhere in the story, his agent offers an explanation: the troubled athlete never got over the death of his older brother six years earlier. . . . On television, we watch the commemoration of the attack on the World Trade Center. Those who mourn the victims rise to read the names of the deceased. The fourth year following the tragedy, sibling survivors are the designated readers. A sister is mentioned, a brother's name recited in a tremulous voice.

Scanning the morning paper, I am drawn to the letters to the editor section, where I come upon the following: "My brother died an untimely death at age 32—17 months ago—and yet my first thought every day is 'he's still dead.'" I am so moved by the letter that I locate and telephone its author, Erin St. John Kelly. We meet (see Chapter 3) and embrace each other. Though our stories are different, circumstances of life and death are different, relationships to our deceased siblings are different, she and I are kindred spirits.

Surviving siblings need to have their loss validated, to be recognized as mourners. "When my brother died, none of my friends came to the funeral," I am told by a woman in her thirties whose older brother died of melanoma four years ago. "They didn't think it was important enough. One of them even said to me, 'Why are you carrying on like this? It's not as if you've lost a parent.' But this was worse than losing a parent. This was my *brother*. I wasn't anybody's kid sister anymore."

The death of a sibling often results in role change, both within the family (a surviving brother might have to assume the role of caretaker to ailing parents, for example, once his sister dies) and without. The surviving sibling in a two-child family put it plainly: "I went from being a sister to being someone who *had* a sister."

A goal of this book is to provide recognition and validation.

Surviving siblings are often expected to put others' needs first. Sometimes it is good to have others to worry about. "When my sister died of a heart attack at age forty-five (she had *not* been ill), I was, like, beyond in shock," recalls the younger sister, some twenty years after the event. "She was divorced and her kids had no contact with their father. I went home for the funeral and realized that my mother needed me (she had just lost a child), my nieces and nephews needed me (they had just lost their mother), and so I sold my home in Brooklyn and moved back to Michigan with my daughter to be there for everyone." She begins to cry, and says, "I just realized that though everybody needed me, I needed them, too. I still do. I am very close with my sister's kids; they are like my own kids. And I love their children. I just adore them. They are like my grandchildren. That's been the saving grace of all this."

However, other survivors find that focusing on everyone else's needs following the death of their sister or brother keeps them from the important grief work of dealing with their own feelings. "When my brother died in a car accident, everyone asked me, 'How are your parents doing?'" says a younger sister. "But nobody asked how *I* was doing. I did take care of my parents, even moving back home for a year to do so, and I was a wreck."

A man in his sixties recalls: "When my brother died—it was fairly sudden—I couldn't take the time to grieve. I had to comfort my sister-in-law. After all, she was the spouse. I was devastated, but her grief came first."

As a result, this man—like many other surviving siblings who become the protectors of their parents or of the surviving spouse and children of the deceased—was forced to set aside his own mourning.

Kenneth J. Doka, Ph.D., professor of gerontology at The College of New Rochelle and a mental health grief counselor who is also senior consultant to the Hospice Foundation of America, describes this situation—where survivors' loss is unacknowledged and their pain unsupported—as *disenfranchised grief*. If others fail to recognize the importance of the issue, the depth of the loss, the void that has been created when a sibling dies, says Doka, "The first thing for a survivor to do is to validate your own grief, then seek out support."

A goal of this book is to provide support.

There is value in telling the story. In speaking with the many men and women who recalled for me the death of their brother or sister, I am struck by the therapeutic value to survivors of telling the story—not just about how their loved ones died but also how they lived. I ask many questions in the interviews—about family history, relationship to the sibling who died (older? younger? close? distant?). I ask about circumstances of the death, about family and community supports: what helped (sometimes only a friend who held their hand); what hurt (a dismissive comment, something like "You have other brothers and sisters, don't you?"). I seek to identify opportunities they have found for perpetuating the memory of the deceased. ("I *still* question whether I honored my brother's memory sufficiently," I am told by one survivor five years after the death of his brother at the age of forty-seven. "That's probably one of the reasons that I reached out to you.") Survivors feel a need to make some sense of it all, to connect. I speak with siblings who feel strongly that, in one way or other, the deceased person remains present in their lives—sometimes figuratively ("I half expect him to come walking in the door"), sometimes more concretely (see Chapter 11).

We vary in how we grieve. There was a time, not so very long ago in fact, when the following ideas were widely accepted: that we grieve in predictable patterns (the stages identified by Elisabeth Kübler-Ross in connection with the terminally ill—denial, anger, bargaining, depression, and acceptance—were broadly applied to describe a progression for *all* who struggle with issues of loss and mourning); that grief is time-limited; and that resolving one's grief means letting go of the person who died.

Reality presents us with a different picture. Though there are things that grievers feel in common, we now recognize that grief is an individual process—differing even among surviving siblings in the same family, each of whom had a different relationship to the one who died. In addition, points out Sherry Schachter, Ph.D., RN, a respected grief therapist, "Part of how we grieve is based on who we are, our backgrounds, our religious beliefs, our cultural beliefs, the experiences that we've had with death." Some of us are *intuitive grievers*, people who cry, who respond to the loss of a loved one emotionally, and some are *instrumental grievers*, who grieve through acts like setting up a foundation or going on the lecture circuit to speak of the dangers of drunk driving when that was the cause of death. "There are also individuals who go back and forth, who do both (respond emotionally and practically)," says Schachter. "It's a continuum."

The stories you will find here reflect that variety and can be therapeutic for us all. If you are reading this book, chances are that you're a member of the survivor community (or you care about someone who has been devastated by the loss of a sibling). Though every situation has its uniqueness and every relationship its own nuances, I hope you will find (as I did) commonalities in the diversity of these stories that affirm your own feelings, insights that deepen your understanding, and suggestions that point the way to healing.

There is value, I believe, in hearing others' stories. For this reason, many of the experiences recounted by survivors are reported in these pages at some length.

Some of the people who spoke with me agreed to be identified. Where that is the case, first and last names are given. For those who requested anonymity, only first names are used and are altered, although the actual statements and circumstances are accurately presented. I have placed the various case histories throughout the narrative. Inevitably, there are crossovers from chapter to chapter. As you use the book, please also check out sections that do not obviously relate to you. A memory, a phrase, an observation may find a place in your heart, may help you move forward. The insights of one or another of the professionals who share their wisdom in these pages may also help.

This book is about communication. My hope is that it provides not just a better understanding of sibling grief but a better understanding, for all of us, of how to support survivors of any kind of loss.

The loss is enduring. "I have a friend who keeps telling me that time heals all wounds," says a grieving sister. "I hate it when she tells me that. Losing my sister was like having my arm cut off. A whole part of me is gone. Forever."

"I hear this from many siblings, that this wasn't just another person who died but this was part of me," says Rabbi Simcha Weintraub, a grief specialist who directs the National Center for Jewish Healing. "They're grieving for part of themselves. That's why it is so painful that the loss is not taken seriously enough... because it is incredibly profound, and in order to move ahead you need to be able to name that and talk about it and work it through somehow."

It used to be thought that one "gets over" a death. Current understanding of the grief process, however, holds that it is not time-limited. We continue to miss the siblings who have left us, as the following excerpt makes clear.

"My mother's next younger sister, Fanny, is now a very fragile old lady," wrote anthropologist Margaret Mead in her memoir, *Blackberry Winter*.[1] "She lives in a nursing home where she still entertains her

---

friends and relatives at cocktails. . . . She is ninety-five, and seeing her so gay and so aware of the world around her gives an extraordinary pleasure to her nieces, her grandnieces, and her great-grandnieces. But she still laments that her sister Emily, my mother, is not with her to share her last years."

Mead had herself lost a sister, Katherine, who died in her first year of life. "I knew she had died," Mead wrote, "but my lost little sister lived on in my daydreams."

One does not get over the death of a sibling, one gets through it. But the loss is enduring.

Yes, life goes on for us survivors.

But differently.

CHAPTER 1

Siblings: A Complex Relationship

Brothers and sisters strongly influence our lives.

Psychologist Victor Cicirelli, a leading researcher into sibling relationships, has described the sibling tie as unique among human relationships in its duration, its egalitarianism, and its sharing of a common heritage. Most siblings, he found, maintain some contact with each other until the end of their lives.

The relationship is also uniquely complicated.

A story is told of a firstborn's reaction to the birth of a sibling. The child is elated, stands at cradle's side, and rocks the infant ever so gently back and forth. The parents look on, beaming. After a week or so of tolerance, even mild interest in the visitor, the older child informs his parents that it's okay, the newborn can go back to the hospital—only to learn that this gift is nonreturnable. "You mean she's staying?!" asks the firstborn with obvious dismay.

Only time will tell if the gift is welcome.

But the identity of the two children has already been affected: firstborn becomes "big brother," the younger child "kid sister." As they grow up, both will continue to see themselves in these roles. When I ask surviving siblings to describe the makeup of their family of origin, for example, many employ these terms of connection. The youngest of three brothers, now in his sixties, still describes himself to me as "the baby in the family."

Our siblings define us. "Our siblings frame our identity," says Ken Doka, Ph.D., whose several identities include Lutheran minister, grief counselor, professor, and author. Still, "Part of who I'll always be is

Dotty and Frankie's kid brother," he says. *We see ourselves in relationship to our siblings. When they die, we may have to reinvent ourselves.*

Our parents define us. But there is more than birth order involved in the differentiation process: the way we feel about our "self" that emerges in relation to a sibling. We are also greatly influenced by our parents' view of us. In *Original Kin*, her book about the search for connection among adult brothers and sisters, Marian Sandmaier points out, "Many of us are given several roles [by our parents] along different dimensions, including achievement (the scholar, the artist, the jock); behavior (the devil, the angel, the loner, the clown); and family function (the caretaker, the peacemaker, the scapegoat). . . . "

We define ourselves. Add to that the competition we each engage in as we seek to distinguish ourselves from our siblings. In my own case, as last-born child (the baby in the family), I grew up with a strong awareness that my sister Sybil was immensely popular. She had a winning smile and welcoming personality. More than anything, she loved to dance—fox trot, jitterbug, rumba—and never lacked for partners. My brother Sam, on the other hand, was a born leader—head of one or another club and student organization. In light of their attainments, which I greatly admired, how could I hope to distinguish myself? Then I entered school and found sure footing. As I brought home my end-term reports, I remember thinking, *Well, here's one area where* I'm *the star.*

The point is: I identified with my siblings and evaluated my achievement *in terms of theirs.* What I was doing in marking out my own arena is known as *deidentification*—the motivation to become someone different from them, to be my own person. Says Sandmaier, "The more sisters and brothers one has, the more picking and choosing [among traits] takes place, with each sibling offering different, critical pieces of information about who to be—or not to be."

Sometimes we may strive to be different from our siblings because of traits that we view as negative. "My brother has *always* been lazy," says a go-getter, "whereas I'm the kind of guy who turns in special reports for extra credit." Again, the speaker's industriousness is viewed by him as a *response* to his brother's lassitude. The message? "He may be my brother, but here's how we differ."

Sandmaier writes, "As models and allies, and as warnings and foils, sisters and brothers do nothing less than help us create ourselves." Note that the standard of comparison is centered on our siblings. Our goal is to shape up to or surpass our sister or brother, not the kid next door.

Often overlooked in all the talk of rivalry between siblings is a significant advantage they enjoy in not being the only child in the family.

As Stephen P. Bank and Michael D. Kahn point out in their important work, *The Sibling Bond*, "Each child absorbs a unique blend of what the parents love and hate about themselves.... The advantage of having siblings is that no one child has to be the sole bearer of the family projection process." It is easier for us to meet parental expectations when they are spread among several children: for example, the social child, the leader, the student. Fortunately for the three children in my family, our parents were not dead set on raising an athlete.

Further, in divvying up the turf ("She's the athlete; he's the studious one"), siblings often lessen the rivalry and pave the way for greater acceptance and friendship. We may start out feeling hostile toward a sibling, we may have ambivalent relationships (loving and hating), but most of us come around to making peace with and valuing the relationship.

I witnessed this not only in my family of origin but also in the family my husband, Noel, and I created. Our first two sons were at odds with each other from the afternoon when Mitch toddled into Eric's room and destroyed the building-block raceway that Eric, three years older, had laboriously constructed. From that time and for years thereafter, "Stay out of my room" was an oft-repeated admonishment used by either brother. But Eric was devoted to his best friend, Greg, who was always welcome in his room. It was Greg this and Greg that, while Mitch was *persona non grata*.

One day, I took my older son aside. "Listen," I said, "Greg is a great kid and I'm glad that you two get along so well. But look ahead. You and Greg are likely to go off to different schools, to develop different interests. Who knows if this friendship will last until adulthood. One thing, however, is certain. Mitchell will continue to be your brother for the rest of your life. You can have him as an enemy or as a friend. Friend is better."

Today, both Eric and Mitch are married and live in different parts of the world, yet they call each other frequently, speak as well to their younger brother, Orin, and enjoy getting together whenever possible—notably at family gatherings. Their sibling relationship satisfies Cicirelli's criteria of duration, egalitarianism, and the sharing of a common heritage. That they are also friends is a bonus. (Note: Eric and Greg remain friendly as well.)

Custodians of family history: "Sisters and brothers share what no other contemporaries can share: the intimate, resonant details of family history," writes Judith Viorst in her book, *Necessary Losses*. "This sharing, if we are able to get past the rivalry, can lay the foundation of a lifetime connection, a connection that can sustain us though parents die and children leave—and marriages fail."

Bank and Kahn found that sisters tend to have closer relationships with one another than brothers. "Women are most often the ones who initiate communication, remembrances, and family get-togethers," they explain. "But it is interesting that while men tend not to speak about their feelings with their brothers and sisters, they often hold sentiments of value just as deeply."

This distinction between the sexes is not borne out by interviews with the men and women in this study. Both groups were candid, introspective, emotional, articulate. For both, the relationship with the deceased was significant and the loss immeasurable. There was, however, one noteworthy difference. Women who spoke of their grief had lost either a brother or sister; with one exception the men spoke only about brothers who died. That may be because sisters have either a nurturing feeling (for a younger brother) or a worshipful feeling (toward an older one). Or it may be because women are more likely to want to talk about their feelings—that they are intuitive mourners—than are men.

For both men and women, however, the sibling relationship can be profoundly important and the death of a sibling both complex and crushing.

"When I lost my sister, I lost someone who loved me unconditionally," I am told by a sixty-year-old woman whose sister died of cancer ten years earlier. "I have never filled that void."

And a man who was more distantly connected to an older sibling laments, "When my brother died, I lost the only person who could verify my family history—someone I could call and ask, 'What year did we move to the house on Elm Street?' Now that may not seem important, but it is. Part of my past died with my brother, and it hurts."

"Our siblings really matter to us throughout life," says David Fireman, executive director of the Center for Grief Recovery, located in Chicago. "Our lives are shaped by them: from whom we choose to hang out with, the quality of our relationships, the work we do—those influences go back to our sibling bonds in ways that we have yet to really discover. Unfortunately, it is not until somebody loses a sibling that they begin to take stock of that. Because it's not identified as primary loss. And yet it *is* primary."

That is why we grieve when our sister or brother dies. And why, no matter when or how it happens, it seems to us too sudden and too soon.

Sister

she was supposed to die slowly
in a starring role
getting more wrinkled moving less fast
turning her head at an angle
as my father does now
to pick up softer parts of conversations
laugh a half second later than others
when the joke made its way to her

she was supposed to take her time
to sit more
and watch more
and be more quiet
to have the luxury
of bitching about her conditions
and laughing with that disgusted smirk
she used so often on democrats
and others with no class or taste

instead:
she went in fast forward
gone at 52
and the speed of it all
is taking us aback

wait a minute:
start the film over
let her have a few more reels

it seems she was
just coming to another subplot
when the credits came on
the lights came up
and we were made to usher ourselves out
the quiet shuffle of feet
betraying our own existence
in our horrid disbelief
that the movie had had its run.

—John Sherman, "Finis"

Reprinted by permission of the author.

CHAPTER 2

And Then There Was One

The silver-framed photograph shows two teenage girls. The younger—with blond bangs, hair held back in a ponytail—looks directly at the camera. She's dressed in a cheerleader's uniform, scarlet and gold, and is smiling broadly. The older girl, slightly taller and also fair, wears her hair in a shorter style and her expression is more contained. Sporting a pink shirt and navy cardigan, she is turned slightly and her arm is slung lightly across the younger girl's shoulders.

"That's us—sisters," says Marcia, now thirty, the older of the two. She was seventeen then, in her last year of high school, and Patty, her kid sister and only sibling, barely fifteen. "Patty and I used to do everything together—ice-skating, watching TV, going to movies, just hanging out," she says. "We were joined at the hip." Two weeks after the photo was taken, Patty was diagnosed with rhabdomyosarcoma, a fast-growing, highly malignant tumor that usually affects young children. "The doctor explained that Patty's chances of beating the aggressive cancer were small, say 13 percent, because she was in very good health when the disease struck," says Marcia. "I clung to the words 'very good health' and refused to believe that my sister could die."

At Patty's insistence, Marcia went away to college that fall as planned. "It's like I led two lives," she says. "When I was at school I was a student. When I went home I dealt with a sister who was very, very sick." She was home for the summer, working in a local supermarket, when Patty lapsed into a coma and died.

And Marcia, then nineteen, went from being big sister to only child.

SUDDENLY ONLY

When parents die, the adult child (no matter how old) faces the realization of being an orphan. When death takes a brother or sister, the surviving sibling also has a change in status. This transition is keenly felt by those who are "suddenly only" (as contrasted with children who grow up as only children, never having looked to a sister or brother for companionship and caring). It should be no surprise that the number of men and women in this situation is growing.

In her book, *In the Presence of Grief*, social worker Dorothy Becvar addresses the phenomenon, noting that (for a variety of reasons) families tend to be smaller today than was previously the case. "Parents are likely to feel complete, as well as safe, with the arrival of their desired one or two children," she says. Given the trend to smaller families, she points out, "Not only is the death of a child a great shock to everyone involved, but for the brother or sister it may mean the loss of one's sole sibling." The only remaining partner for the surviving child in the ongoing effort to define oneself within family is, in Becvar's words, "the ghost of the dead sister or brother."

As a survivor, Marcia went largely unseen. "My family was flooded with sympathy cards, but they were all addressed to my parents," she says. "And people I met around town kept asking me how my mom and dad were doing—not a word about whether *I* was okay." Back at school, she also found little sympathy. "The people in my dorm, in my classes, in my sorority evaded the issue, and that was very difficult for me," she recalls. "I felt as if the responsibility lay with me to help *them* avoid any discomfort, so on the rare occasion when someone asked about my sister I'd quickly change the subject. It took me a while to realize that my friends weren't saying anything because nobody close to them had died and they didn't know what to say."

Emotional stress often shows up as a physical problem. Marcia began to experience dizzy spells and made an appointment at the student health center. "I don't remember what I was asked," she says, "but I told the doctor about Patty. . . . I must have told her a lot (finally, somebody was interested in how I was doing) because she arranged for me to speak with a therapist—someone who was very helpful and whom I saw for many years."

WHEN SIBLINGS DIE YOUNG: GRIEVING A LOST FUTURE—THEIRS AND YOURS

As has been noted, the death of a sibling is the loss of one's past, of one's present, and of expectations one has for the future. This is especially true when siblings die young. As Yann Martel sensitively observes in his moving novel, *Life of Pi*, "To lose a brother [in this case, one whose life lay largely ahead] is to lose someone with whom you can share the experience of growing old, who is supposed to bring you a sister-in-law and nieces and nephews, creatures to people the tree of your life and give it new branches."

Similarly, Marcia is struggling to make peace with changed expectations. "When I used to think of myself as an adult, I'd just picture that I'd be living with my sister," she says. "It's very weird. I wanted to get married and have kids. Patty and I used to leaf through bridal magazines, choosing our gowns, our wedding rings, our china. But I'd also think, well, when I graduate from college, I'll get a job and Patty and I will have an apartment together. We'll do this together and we'll do that together. There'll be time later to settle down. She was just part of my future, and that future died with her. I don't know if there's any connection between that and the fact that I'm still single. I may even now be looking for the carefree existence that I thought I'd enjoy with Patty."

NEW ROLE, NEW RESPONSIBILITIES

Reality has presented Marcia with a different picture.

"The loss of an only sibling is devastating," says P. Gill White, Ph.D., surviving sibling, therapist, and author of *Sibling Grief*. "If that happens and you still have parents, then you're now the one who has to take care of everything—from giving them grandchildren to caring for them in their old age."

For Marcia at thirty, an age when most people are blissfully unencumbered by caregiving concerns, these issues are a serious consideration because she is well aware that, when the time comes, she will have to shoulder the responsibility for her parents on her own. For several years, she stayed on and worked as a teacher in the city where she'd attended college. Recently, however, she has moved back to her hometown to offer an extra pair of hands in caring for an ailing grandfather and to be a company keeper for her mother and father.

For this only child, working with a professional counselor—having someone to talk to—remains critical to the recovery process. "When my sister died, I lost my confidante," she says. "So if my mother gets on my nerves, I don't have anybody to share that with. But if my sister were here, I could say, 'Oh, Lord, she's driving me crazy,' and my sister would understand. Or if my dad is bugging me, I can't really talk to my mother about it. And I do have issues with my parents. They keep asking me where I'm going, who I'm seeing, and when I expect to be home. I remind them that I lived away for twelve years, and if I was living away now they wouldn't know whether I was out or not. They're being super protective because I'm the only one left. I can, and do, discuss these issues in therapy. Eleven years have gone by since my sister died, and I'm still dealing with the consequences of her death."

FINDING ANOTHER PERSON WHO EXPERIENCED SIGNIFICANT LOSS IS HELPFUL

The task is lightened when it is shared, and Marcia feels fortunate to have lately reconnected with an old acquaintance, someone she grew up with and now values as a friend. "She was in her early twenties when her father committed suicide," Marcia tells me. "We enjoy doing things together, but we can also talk about family stuff. She's very sensitive about fathers and she knows about sibling relationships because she has a brother—an only brother. It's never a matter between us of whose loss is harder to take. It's nice to talk to someone else who has experienced a very significant loss and who has found a way to live and move on."

Survivors who are "suddenly only" when a sibling dies do well to reach out to others—friends, family members, fellow mourners, grief counselors—for support on the journey. Being only does not have to translate into being alone.

ADDRESSING ALTERED RELATIONSHIPS WITH ONE'S PARENTS

Where Marcia has basically had to grow up without her sister, Anita LaFond Korsonsky became an only child in mid-life when on September 11, 2001, her sister Jeanette, who was four years younger, died at the age of forty-nine in the terrorist attack on the World Trade Center. Jeanette worked on the ninety-fourth floor of the first tower. (The story of the sisters, and the challenges of mourning someone who has died in the public eye, are discussed at greater length in Chapter 6.) Though the details of life, circumstances of death, and support systems available to Anita and Marcia are different, I am drawn to the similarities between Marcia's experience and the emotions and life changes described by Anita.

Like Marcia, Anita has found it helpful to seek professional support in dealing with the void created by her sister's death. "I could share things with my sibling—different things about my mom or my dad or about whatever else is happening in life," she says. "When you're talking to a sibling, you talk about things that took place when you were growing up, funny things that happened or maybe not-so-funny things. When they die, that relationship no longer exists. Of course I can discuss things with my husband or other family members, but it's not the same. They don't have the growing-up experience of how to deal with a certain situation. It's not like, 'Well, you know that Mom was always like this.' That connection, that immediate understanding, is gone forever. The relationship with my sister ended and all the memories reside within me and with no one else. And because I don't have another sibling, I can't say to a brother or another sister, 'Remember when the three of us did this.'"

Like Marcia, Anita has been challenged by the changed relationship with her parents—specifically, her mother (her father died ten months after Jeanette was killed). "I'd never had to deal with my mom as an only child, and the whole dynamic between us instantly changed," Anita says. "For example, when my sister was around, I didn't necessarily call my mother every day. Jeanette was closer to our mother, and I knew she would phone her every morning when she got to work and each evening when she got home. *I* do that now. I don't know if it's because I'm concerned about my mother, who is an extremely capable person, or it's a case of my sister did this so I should do it now. My mom and I both have memories of somebody—her daughter, my sister—who no longer exists. We continue to work on building a new connection without her.

"It's a lot to carry around," Anita says. "It could make you crazy if you didn't understand how to deal with it. I asked the therapist if it was okay to have these feelings. She said, 'Yes, as long as you're functioning with your life.'"

"WE DIDN'T GET ALONG BUT . . . "

To this point, the focus has been on those survivors for whom the person who died played two roles: sibling and best friend. Indeed, for most of the people you will meet in this book, men and women who have outlived a sister or brother, the themes of love and loss are closely intertwined. I find it easy to make a connection to these mourners because, like them, I grieve the loss of someone who was both sister and best friend. But what if there's not that closeness, I wonder. Is the loss of an only sibling still significant?

Cara begins the interview with a disclaimer: "My sister and I were not close, so I don't know if you'll find what I have to say very helpful."

A tall woman, slim, dark-haired, high-cheekboned, Cara holds herself erect in the way of people who have studied dance. She did dance, she tells me, although she makes her living as a physical therapist. She's fifty-five, two years younger than Halley, her late sister and only sibling.

"My sister, as I was growing up, was someone that I looked up to," Cara says. "She was very smart, but she had a volatile temper so I was somewhat afraid of her. When we were children, we did not play together. Then we grew up and our lives took different paths. She was a reader, I was a dancer. We moved to opposite parts of the country. In our twenties, thirties, and early forties, we'd see one another on occasion—generally at family get-togethers—but we'd still speak to each other fairly often. We had a similar sense of humor so that we could call and say zany things to one another that, really, only she and I would understand because of being sisters and having grown up together. . . . However, she was problematic to me. Eventually, we had nothing to do with one another."

It wasn't a matter of simply drifting apart. A disciplined person, Cara disapproved of Halley's casual lifestyle, of her reliance on alcohol to deal with her problems. Halley felt that Cara had been insufficiently involved with their ailing parents. (Their mother is no longer living.) Harsh words were said. Then they stopped talking. Completely. Three years into the breakup, Cara got a call from her father who told her that Halley was dying. The cause was liver and kidney failure.

With Halley's death, Cara became an only child. "*That*," she says with some surprise, "is the hardest thing for me. I'm still in a bit of a shock that my sister *has* died. It is so difficult for me. . . . I actually have a physical sense . . . I mean, physically there's something different . . .

there's something missing. No matter what happened, she was part of me. Even though I have a husband and I have good friends, there is the sense that I have physically lost something. You know, this person that I expected to be in my life... certainly for many years into the future... I feel that we have been cut off from that future, she and I, and that I am alone."

"When your sister died, how did people respond to you?" I ask.

"When my mother died, I received many letters and notes of condolence," Cara replies. "When my sister died, there were very few. I don't know why that is exactly, although I think that because of the circumstances of my sister's death, people did not know how to respond. It was very sudden. She died of a disease that is not socially acceptable. It was hard for people to talk about it. And then there's the fact that she and I were estranged. With the death of my mother, people said, 'I am sorry for your loss.' When my sister died, what they said to me was, 'I don't know how to respond.'

"And I didn't know what to tell them."

LOOKING FOR ANSWERS AT AL-ANON HELPS

"The biggest thing that has been helpful to me is that I've begun going to Al-Anon meetings," Cara says. "I go very diligently. I am so angry with my sister. I'm so angry about how she abused her body. I'm angry that she didn't come to me. I'm furious that she died."

Anger is a frequent emotion for survivors, who feel a need to rail against someone, something, especially when the death is untimely or, as in Halley's case, brought on by her own behavior. To cope with her anger, Cara is trying to understand that behavior, to make some sense of it all. "Attending these meetings for family and friends of alcoholics and reading the Al-Anon literature has been a godsend," she says. "There's a lot of behavior that Halley exhibited... well, her whole life... and I've been trying to understand the why in all that. I've come to appreciate that the disease of alcoholism was so advanced that, in a way, the why doesn't even matter. I find an incredible amount of information and support in the group.

"You know," Cara says, "I have these photographs of my sister and me and I look at these pictures, and I'm trying to remember a time when she and I were in a more meaningful relationship. I'm really trying to reconnect with my sister. I wish I could tell her that."

BECOMING AN ONLY CHILD IN THE LATER YEARS

One doesn't have to grow up in a two-child family to be left suddenly only by a sibling's death. A year ago, shortly after celebrating his seventieth birthday, Norman became an only child. The youngest of three sons, he had grown up somewhat in the shadow of his oldest brother Harold ("the athlete"), seven years his senior, and Ben ("the scientist"), three years older. In this family of achievers, Norman distinguished himself as the most social and outgoing ("the politician"). The brothers grew up, married, had children and grandchildren, and remained close. They would speak to each other at least once a week, see each other once or twice a month, get together at holiday and family celebrations.

Four years ago, Harold died after a long battle with prostate cancer. The younger brothers were sad, but the loss was anticipated—they'd done some of their mourning as they traveled together to pay frequent visits to their dying big brother. "Harold's decline definitely brought Ben and me closer," Norman says. "After he died, we would call each other often and trade Harold stories: 'Remember when he did this'... 'Remember how he used to do that.' To tell the truth, I was sad when Harold died, but the impact of losing a sibling was not so obvious to me. There were still Ben and myself. We had each other for support."

One year ago Ben developed pneumonia and died quickly and quite suddenly. "And *then* it hit me," says Norman. "I was now alone."

In a society that pays too little attention to sibling loss in general, the impact of becoming "only" in one's later years is pretty much ignored. All too frequently, the grief goes unrecognized and the mourner unsupported. Says counselor Ken Doka, "If you're seventy-two years old and your seventy-year-old brother dies, people are going to focus on the widow. They're going to focus on the adult children, even the grandchildren, not on you, although you've lost someone who has been important to you for seventy years!"

"One of the biggest problems for older people is grief," says P. Gill White. "They've lost so much." Norman now finds himself mourning the deaths of both of his brothers.

"After Ben died I really did for the first time come to terms with the several losses," he says. "The ability to pick up a phone and check in, to take note of an old family relationship, to pass along a joke or anecdote, there is no opportunity to do that anymore. That had a real impact on me.... It still does. There's the feeling of no longer being connected to what had been a reasonably close family. There is a void. I don't know if I would describe it as grieving, but there sure is a void."

It's the void that Marcia feels... that Anita understands... that Cara describes as a kind of physical assault. An emptiness to which attention must be paid.

CHAPTER 3

"But You Have Other Siblings, Don't You?"

> My brother died an untimely death at age 32—17 months ago—and yet my first thought every day is "he's still dead." He was 10 years younger than I, and was the fourth of six children. When he died, I didn't feel as if anyone who hadn't lost a sibling could understand the particular grief I felt. Among the useless consolations offered were "but you come from a big family, right?" or "you have another brother, don't you?"
>
> —Erin St. John Kelly, in a letter to *The New York Times*

"Our siblings are *not* interchangeable," Erin declares forcefully when we meet. That being said, those who grow up in a multichild family often find that when a sibling dies they can and do turn to one another in their grief. Unlike siblings who find themselves "suddenly only" following the death of a sister or brother, they are not alone. The ability to find support within the family, however, does not lessen the grief felt when a brother or sister dies. Each member of a family has a unique relationship to the others. For each, then, the loss is differently felt. The loss must be recognized and honored.

The oldest of eight in a yours, mine, and ours family created by the multiple marriages of her parents, Erin doted on her younger brother, James. (They share the same mother.) "I'd say he was my first baby," says Erin, forty-two, married and the mother of two daughters. "I remember him in diapers; I remember dressing him in his little outfits; I remember pushing him in his stroller up and down the driveway. Then, when he grew up, he became the kind of person *I* could depend on. He was earnest, a truth teller, and he was very gentle. He was our emotional center; he linked the families."

On a Sunday in October, Erin received an anguished call from her mother, telling her that James had died. How could that be? She knew that James and his wife, Tara, were traveling on a humanitarian mission around the world. That was so like her kid brother. What she now heard was something she could never imagine: This same young and vigorous man had become ill with altitude sickness in a small town in Bolivia, suffered a pulmonary edema, and died.

Within hours of the call, Erin made plans to link up with another brother, Chris, and fly to Bolivia, meeting up with James's wife. Together they went to the funeral parlor, saw James's body, and arranged for him to be cremated. "It has since been important that I saw him because I could then dispel any hope—any strange kind of fantasizing—that he was still alive, that he was just off on another long trip," Erin says.

FINDING COMFORT IN FAMILY

The surreal nature of the event followed Erin home. "The hard part initially was that, wherever I went, I felt I had this awful secret," she says. "If I told people that my brother died, it would just ruin everyone else's good time. I had something nobody else could process, which is why I wanted to hang out with my family."

There was another reason. "After James died it made me realize that I hadn't been paying as much attention to him and maybe *all* my siblings as I thought I had. Because I started thinking back to events in our past and wondering: *Where was James then? What was going on with James while I was doing this or that?* And then I'd think: *Well, I was growing up, too.* And growing up is a pretty egomaniacal thing. Certainly, going to Bolivia and finding my brother dead and not being able to fix it was the biggest comeuppance in my life."

Though looking forward to going home, she was a little uneasy about it as well. "I thought, *We're all going to be so sad and it will be awful.* But once I got there, to be among my family was actually fantastic. And I think everybody felt that way. Even though James meant different things to each of us, we were all mourning our brother. One of my sisters wrote a poem on the anniversary of his death, and in it she had one line that said, 'I still count you as one of my brothers.' But that's a weird transition, too. Am I the oldest of eight or am I now the oldest of seven? I have to redefine that.

"I need James's death to be less fresh," Erin says. "But as it becomes less fresh, it brings its own sorrow and guilt. I want him to be as vivid for me as he was the day he died."

AS IF IT WERE YESTERDAY . . .

I wish that Erin could meet Marybeth Wahle, who is much further along in her grief journey and thus could provide her with helpful perspective and support. Like Erin, Marybeth experienced the devastating and untimely death of a much-loved sibling when her brother Michael died in a freak accident at the age of twenty-one, some thirty years ago. Like her, she has had the good fortune to be able to find comfort in family even as that family was diminished by the loss of one of its own.

"I have since gone on to lead a very good life," Marybeth tells me, "but the loss of my close sibling (both in age and in heart) has in many, many ways shaped who I am and has given me a different lens on life and a feeling for others who suffer." Married, with four children and a career as the head of her own public relations firm, Marybeth, fifty-two, made time in her schedule to share her story because, she said, "If anything you write on this subject helps somebody, I'm in."

Thirty years ago: Marybeth grew up in West Hartford, Connecticut, as the fourth of five children—all born within six years of one another. "My childhood was a total gift," she says. "The older I get, the more I realize how lucky we were." She was a senior at the College of the Holy Cross in Worcester, Massachusetts, when her brother Michael (just shy of a year and a half older than she) dropped by. He was on his way to Cape Cod to attend the wedding of one of his best friends. "So I sat and visited with him and some of my friends and watched him walk away to go to this wedding," Marybeth says. "The next morning, I got a phone call from one of my sisters. She was crying and crying, and I thought for a moment that my grandmother, who'd been ill, must have died. Then she finally got the words out of her mouth: *Michael drowned.* And I said, 'What are you talking about? No way!' I still recall when I heard the words in my ear and felt that there was shaking in my brain.

"What happened was, he was at a rehearsal dinner for his friend the night before the wedding. The restaurant was at the water's edge. As I understand it, the room got filled with smoke and he went out to walk on a pier. Had it been daylight, he would have seen that the pier was very rickety. Either the pier caved in or he fell from it. He hit his head and was knocked unconscious and drowned.

"After I received the news, a couple of my college friends drove me home, and for a split second on the ride I wished that I could be in a car crash so I could be with him . . . which sounds so irrational, but at the time I thought, *He's alone, he's alone.* I didn't want him to be alone. I don't think I slept or stopped crying for days."

Early stages—what helped, what hurt: The initial time was a blur. But certain people and their acts of understanding and kindness stand out vividly for Marybeth to this day. "I do remember the brother of a friend of mine coming in, sitting down, and just holding my hand. I didn't have to talk to him. He was just there for me. I've never forgotten that."

When Marybeth returned to school, she found herself unable to focus on her studies or participate in student life. "Kids were having Halloween parties and I couldn't get through the day," she says. "As the term unfolded, I remember realizing: I'm not on the same planet as these people anymore and never will be. After a few weeks, I felt that I had to leave school and go home. Then a friend of my sister told me, 'This may sound harsh, but you're going to have to figure a way to go on or you're not going to graduate with your class. Michael wouldn't have wanted that.' I knew she was right, so I went back to school again.

"While no loss is a good loss, a sudden loss conjures up thoughts of *Did I say everything? Did I do everything?* Because I didn't have the chance to say goodbye. I have always considered it a huge gift that my college roommate and my other best friend who lived down the hallway had both suffered sudden losses, though in each case of their fathers, and helped me get through day to day. Remember, this was at a time when grief counseling was unheard of, so being able to talk to friends was extremely important. For example, I was having nightmares and my roommate would say, 'Hey, we're sleeping with the light on.' And it actually helped. She had a car at school. One day she put her keys down and said, 'These are here. If you ever feel the need to go home, I'll either drive you or you take the car if you're able.' Things like that were extraordinarily helpful to me.

"There were hurtful things as well," she says. "I remember being back at school and struggling to study, and one young man saying, 'You've got to stop this. You're just feeling sorry for yourself.' And I looked at him in shock, thinking, *No kidding. One of the people who meant most to me has just been ripped out of my life without a chance to say goodbye*. Yes, I felt sorry."

Grief is for the long haul: "I think people don't realize that grief is not one-size-fits-all," says Marybeth. "It's an individual thing, and people grieve differently. Grief is for the long haul. It's like a river. Sometimes it's raging. Sometimes it's kind of quiet, just turning around the bend, but it goes on. Sometimes people are told or will say to themselves, *Okay, it's been a year. Move on.* Frankly, the second year after Michael's death was harder than the first. The first year, you brace yourself for every anniversary or every holiday. The second year, you realize that life will go on without him, and that realization of the permanence of it all was sadder to me—realizing that I would never see my brother married, never see his children born, nor would he be part of events in my life. My wedding day was very hard for me. All of these life events, he wasn't going to be there.

"Sometimes people act as if there's a line in the sand, and then you move past it. Or they say that time heals all wounds. That saying bothered me. Don't tell me that time is going to heal this. Yes, time does help with your ability to cope, but it has never fully taken away the sorrow that I have. Almost thirty years later, I hear a song or I see something that reminds me of him, and I'll be in tears in a split second. Actually, that's a good thing. It's a reminder of how much I loved him."

Thirty years ago, in fact, the traditional view of grieving *did* draw a kind of line in the sand. It viewed grief as a process leading toward some kind of resolution, after which survivors were expected to be "over their grief" and move on. Our current understanding of the ways in which people cope with a significant loss is very different.

"People don't *resolve* grief," says Phyllis Silverman, Ph.D., a social scientist who specializes in research on bereavement. "I think people make *accommodations.* They find a way of living with their pain, with their angst. It's there, but it's not as prominent. It doesn't dominate their life as much." Providing an example, she continues, "As one father [who lost a child] said to me, 'If I lost my pain, it would be disrespect for my son, because this way I remember him and his focus in the way I live my life.'"

Erin St. John Kelly feels similarly. "What makes me feel better so that I can live with my brother's death is when I try to live the kind of life that he'd be proud of me leading," she says.

Marybeth Wahle has made a like assessment. Her brother's death, she says, "has made me stop and look at each day differently. It isn't just the days going by. It's the knowledge that anything can happen . . . and the question: How do I best use this time?"

Sustained by faith: "I grew up in a Catholic home," says Marybeth, "and since Michael's death I've grown closer to my faith rather than farther apart. Not as a crutch but as a way of life. There's a part in the Catholic Mass where you remember those who have gone before you. I've since lost both my parents, but I usually think of Michael first because he was the first loss."

Among the sibling survivors who share their stories with me, several raise the subject of faith. For some, the death of a sister or brother raised serious religious doubts—even a turning away from God. Still others, like Marybeth, cite saying prayers or drawing upon religious faith as an important means of coping. In faith, they find resiliency; in community they find support.

Living with his death, celebrating his life: "The goal of grieving is not to let go but to find a way to hold on with less pain and to have recourse to comforting memory," says Robert Neimeyer, Ph.D., a psychologist at the University of Memphis who has researched and written widely on death and grief and the ways we can cope with loss.

He might well have been speaking of Marybeth and the place she is at today. On what would have been the twentieth anniversary of Michael's death, for example, she put together a video of his life, including photographs of her brother at different times and music from his favorite songs. "The family had a Mass and then a party," she says. "Friends who had gone to high school with him came, and we just chatted about him. And that felt good. . . . No matter how much time goes by, it's important for survivors to talk about the person who has died, *especially* if you lose a sibling . . . because it's not the natural order of things. You expect to lose your parents ahead of you, but you don't expect—especially at a young age—to lose a sibling."

It took Mike Trainor, whom we meet next, a while to acknowledge the depth and duration of his grief.

A TALE OF FOUR BROTHERS

In the beginning there were four brothers—Brian, Mike, David, and Jeff—growing up in Barrington, Rhode Island. "We were what you envision as the typical American family," says Mike, looking back at a carefree, happy childhood. "Then, on an October night four years ago, my brother Brian went to sleep and never woke up. The cause was an arrhythmia, a form of cardiac death. He was thirty-two years old."

Only eighteen months apart, Mike and his older brother attended the same schools, played on the same teams, shared an apartment with some friends for a few years following college. Even after Mike married and moved down South, they kept in close touch. Just two days before Brian died, Mike had come up north from his home in Florida and visited his brother in Boston, where Brian worked as a doctor. "We went to a bar and watched the Red Sox win the World Series," he says. "The guy I left that evening was perfectly healthy—an athlete, six feet tall, a hundred and eighty pounds, someone in great shape. When my youngest brother phoned with news that the State Police had called to inform him that Brian died . . . well, I never really understood the phrase 'hit like a ton of bricks' until that phone call. I kept saying, 'It's gotta be wrong. This can't be true.' But it was."

Newly positioned as the oldest son, Mike quickly took over: selecting a casket, choosing a grave site, making the funeral arrangements, informing family and friends. "You get into more of a doing mode than a grieving mode," he says. "So much needs to be done in such a short time, it's almost cruel. I also felt a big responsibility to be there for my parents—and still do, to a certain extent. The thing that is shocking was that for the first few weeks after Brian's death, I didn't realize its true impact on me."

That came later. "Losing a brother, it's harder than a lot of people realize. Getting together with the family at Christmas or Thanksgiving or a graduation, there are times when you expect him to walk through the door, and it's just not going to happen. Certainly I think of Brian on the anniversary of his death, but for me that's not as challenging as everyday things, the regular reminders that he's not here. Like when the Red Sox were in the playoffs, I would have been on the phone with him three, four times a day, talking about the games. I no longer have that."

IMPORTANCE OF ACKNOWLEDGING THE PAIN

"A few weeks passed, then a few months. I'd think, *Okay, I'm supposed to get up and go to work now, I'm supposed to put a smile on my face. . . .*

Everything just got harder and harder." Mike was experiencing a kind of delayed grieving, which can happen months or even years after the death of the person being mourned. Once the "official" mourning period has passed (and with it the intensive social support of the community), the survivor is left to face the challenge of living day by day without the presence of the one who has died. It is not at all unusual, at this point, for the survivor to experience disorientation and depression. Witnessing Mike's distress, his wife, Katy, suggested that he speak with a counselor.

"It's something I wouldn't see myself doing traditionally," Mike says, "but I had to talk about it with somebody. I picked a name out of the insurance company's directory and made an appointment. By a stroke of luck, the person I'd selected specialized in grief issues."

Everyone who mourns does not necessarily need the services of a counselor, but for some people, like Mike, who find it hard to acknowledge and manage their feelings, such assistance can be very valuable. Says grief specialist Ken Doka, "It can offer validation, it can offer an opportunity to explore the ways you're coping, and it can give you an opportunity to look into some very complicated feelings and emotions you might have. The Association for Death Education and Counseling ["Resources," p. 130] has a list of people who are certified as being specialists in grief."

Mike saw the counselor only three times before he and Katy moved out of state. Still, he found, "Just those three appointments got me on a better path. Turns out, what's helped me the most in coping with my brother's death is talking about it. And I didn't do that, not for a long time. It's very common for men to collect things, keep them on the inside, and not let others know they're in pain."

Research into gender differences in bereavement supports this assessment. "There *are* differences in the way men and women approach things," says Phyllis Silverman. "Women tend to be part of networks more. We tend to be processing our feelings more and have a need to talk to others. So we're less alone than men are. But the research I did showed that men, as they move through the grieving process, often change and become more feeling than they had been, more emotive. They suddenly discover themselves more considerate, more involved with relationships, more committed to nurturing them in ways that they never had noticed before."

Mike's grief journey has followed this trajectory. "After Brian died, there was never a moment when I just lost it and cried for hours," he says. "Instead, whenever the thought of Brian would come into my mind, I would purposely push it away or push it back down into myself. Basically, the counselor spoke with me about the importance of not keeping your emotions or sadness or grieving pushed down into your stomach. He said that you've got to let it out, and once you decide that you're going to grieve about your loss it helps you in the long run. So what I've found helpful is just letting myself think about Brian's death and talking about it with my family.

"I hadn't wanted to bring up the subject with my mom because I feared that it would make her very emotional, but it's turned out to be helpful because she wanted to talk about Brian, too. At family gatherings we now make an effort to tell stories about him, to perpetuate his legacy: 'Oh, Brian would have loved this' . . . 'Brian would be hating this.' Katy and I have a two-year-old daughter, and we tell her she has four uncles—three on my side and one on her mother's side. She recognizes Uncle Brian in photographs. We point him out and she knows who he is. Eventually we'll have to explain that Uncle Brian is in heaven or whatever we'll say."

Like Erin, Mike finds that losing a brother has strengthened the relationship with his remaining siblings. "We've always been close but I know, for me, I value those relationships more now," he says. "I don't think a week goes by that we all don't talk to each other at least once."

FAMILIES UNHAPPY IN THEIR OWN WAY . . .

The loss of a sibling often points up other issues within some large families.

"Following my brother's death, the family dynamics helped in some places and hurt in some places," says Scott Alexander, forty-four, the oldest child in a family that included three brothers (Scott, Stephen, Jamie) and two sisters (Alicia, Ann) who joined them when their mother married the boys' father, Dave, a divorced dad. In 1998, Jamie, then twenty-eight and the family's youngest, met his death in an accident. A hang-gliding instructor, he was taking a student up for a lesson one morning when something went wrong and the glider crashed, killing both young men.

Scott heard the news from his father and quickly flew from his home in Philadelphia to meet with his family and travel to Orlando, Florida, where the accident occurred. "Our being together, talking about Jamie was good," he says. "Going through Jamie's stuff... It was much easier with family members there. But some of the worst of the family dynamics came out also. My parents had never dealt particularly well with each other since the divorce, and so tension that was already there just became worse. Everything was heightened in some way. So there are some good things and some bad things about that."

Being involved in some of the funeral arrangements (Jamie's body was cremated, his ashes were scattered from a hang glider over Biscayne Bay) was useful, says Scott, as was talking with some of his brother's friends. They helped him see a different side of Jamie. Still, he found, "There was a certain weight that stayed with me for a while. There were other stressors. I ended up seeing a therapist (not a grief specialist). Seeing him was helpful in my working through the issues that needed to be worked through."

"Ten years have passed since your brother's death," I say to Scott. "Where are you now?"

"If there is some closeness with my siblings, it's attributable to our being more settled and stable in our lives—not to Jamie's death," he says. "But I do have a closer relationship with my parents, especially with my dad. It's made us realize on both sides that some of the family baggage isn't as important as it felt before."

FINDING COMFORT IN ACTIVISM

Peter, forty-six, describes growing up as the youngest of six—following three older brothers and two sisters. "I'd be lying if I said it was the happiest family in the world," he says. "There certainly were conflicts among the kids and between the parents. Howard, my third brother down, was the only one I got along with. We shared a room when we were children, and used to lie in bed and talk. Though there were six years between us, I considered him my best friend."

Five years ago, Howard died of liver cancer. Although Peter has four surviving siblings, with Howard's death he feels as abandoned as an only sibling. It's not that he and Howard spent that much time together in the last two decades. An avid outdoorsman, Howard had moved out west after college, and infrequent contacts between the two brothers were largely limited to occasional mountain climbing or other adventure expeditions. It's more that Peter had looked to Howard as a kind of anchor to his life—the sole person who understood him and on whom he could depend. With Howard gone, he felt adrift.

Michael D. Kahn, Ph.D., coauthor of *The Sibling Bond*, explains, "When a close relationship with a sibling is forged early in life, then the loss of a brother or sister lingers in the surviving sibling's mind and heart because the identification has been strong: we played together, we laughed together, we fought together. [For Peter, that memory is expressed as "We used to lie in bed and talk."] So when that sibling dies, it's clearly as if a part of oneself is gone. And while people go about their business and go about their lives, it's not to say that they don't feel an emptiness at times because it's as if part of the self has died."

Five years after Howard's death, Peter is still trying to fill that void. His way of doing this and of maintaining the important emotional connection to his brother is by organizing blood drives and otherwise raising public awareness of hemochromatosis, a hereditary condition with which Howard was afflicted and which triggered a number of illnesses he experienced over the years. "With hemochromatosis, high levels of iron start accumulating in a number of body tissues, building up in the vital organs and the joints and all over the body, and failure starts to occur," Peter tells me. "So when Howard was diagnosed with diabetes in his early thirties, he had no idea that there was a connection between the two. He later had problems with his liver, and doctors incorrectly assumed he was an alcoholic. It turns out that if you learn about the condition early and keep your blood levels in check by a simple thing such as donating blood, you're pretty much out of the woods. But the correct diagnosis came too late to help my brother. I was with him when he died of liver cancer. It was a life-altering experience."

SOLACE IN THE SEARCH FOR MEANING

There were four children in Heidi Horsley's family, all born within the space of six years. When Heidi, the oldest, was twenty, her only brother, Scott, was killed in a car accident. Today she holds a doctorate in psychology, a master's degree in social work, she teaches at the Columbia University School of Social Work, is cohost with her mom, Gloria Horsley, of *Healing the Grieving Heart*, an Internet radio show found on www.healthvoiceamerica.com, and also of www.thegriefblog.com. She's now forty-five and lives in New York.

"I absolutely would not be doing what I'm doing today if my brother had not died," she says. "It completely changed the course of my life."

Heidi was a student at the University of Utah when the shocking news reached her. Scott, then seventeen, had been driving in D.C. with a cousin, also seventeen. It was raining. They were going over a bridge when the car hydroplaned, crashed, and blew up. Both boys were killed instantly. Heidi immediately flew to be with her family in upstate New York. In keeping with the by-now-familiar pattern for surviving siblings, she put her grief on hold, focusing instead on caring for her distraught parents and taking over many of their responsibilities, with the notable exception of planning Scott's funeral.

The funeral: Many mourners look back on a funeral or memorial service as having been helpful in the early stages of bereavement. For one thing, it concretizes the death, initiating a formal period of mourning. Further, several survivors cite the requirement to prepare a eulogy—to reflect on the life of the deceased and recall incidents of closeness and connection—as having been beneficial. Heidi experienced Scott's service differently.

"The funeral was not helpful to me because our parents made all the arrangements," she says. "I didn't like the choice of speakers or of music. Neither were representative of my brother. I think siblings need to be consulted. They know the person who died better than anybody. The songs were more religious than his kind of music. I knew Scott's music. I knew his friends. I would have had a little more of who *he* was at the funeral. If I were counseling a parent in this situation, I'd recommend that they ask the siblings if they want to be involved.

"Further, people didn't know what to say to me. Nobody I knew, not one person, had ever had a brother or sister die. They could not begin to understand what that felt like. So they said nothing. And 'nothing' is not helpful. I would have found it better if people had come up to me and said, 'I've never been through this. I don't know what to say.' I'd rather have an acknowledgment than silence. Because I wanted to be able to talk about it and say *Yes, it did happen* over and over and over. It took me a long time to believe that it really did happen even though I knew it did. I would be shocked constantly that Scott was dead."

She also believed that the wrong child was taken.

"My brother carried the family name, he was the only boy, he was very athletic," Heidi says. "The sibling rivalry was more between the girls and we always rallied around him as being the different one. When he died, I felt it should have been me or one of the other girls. Later on, talking to other siblings, I realized that it is not abnormal to feel that way—more particularly because when a sibling dies so much time and energy is spent focusing on that sibling. Further, we tend to talk of the deceased as if they were perfect, no warts. We also seem to remember only the good times. And the family spends a lot of emotional energy grieving their death, they're talked about a lot, there are pictures all over the place, and that can cause you to think even more that the wrong child died. In my case, since it was the only brother who died, I definitely had those thoughts."

Having two surviving siblings definitely helped. "At times they were a great support—especially when our parents were grieving so heavily—because we could talk about how to help them," Heidi says. "I didn't feel the pressure to be everything, the only child. At other times it was painful because there were so many shared memories among us. Sometimes I didn't want to go down those roads. It evoked too much emotion. My sisters are very important to me now. It's interesting because we're very different but we've all filled some of the roles that my brother would have played in the family. I fill the academic role, my sister Rebecca had the first male grandchild and she named him Scott, and my sister Heather is an avid skier, mountain biker, and rock climber, which Scott (who won a lot of awards for athletics) would have appreciated. I've also kept the family name, and my children have hyphenated last names, to perpetuate the connection that would have been carried on by my brother had he lived."

Finding strength to move forward: Following the funeral, Heidi returned to Utah. "I was living halfway across the country from my family, and that was a problem because I had little support," she says. "People at school didn't know my brother. I became extremely depressed. I didn't have passion, meaning, or purpose to my life. I ended up taking a semester off, which was a very good decision. And I went on an Outward Bound program in Colorado. While there, I read Viktor Frankl's book, *Man's Search for Meaning*,[2] and I thought about my own life and about how *did* Frankl survive watching his family die in the Holocaust. I had to know because I didn't know how *I* was going to survive. Reading about Frankl's experience—he had to have a meaning, he had to have a purpose, he had to document the Holocaust so that

[2]This first-person account of Frankl's experiences in the Nazi concentration camps during World War II was mentioned by several surviving siblings as having helped them find new purpose in life.

other people would know what had happened, he had to stay alive so that he could have that documentation—gave me the strength to move forward.

"I had to hear about how other people had managed to live on after they'd lost a sibling. I looked for people who were further along in the grief process to find out: How did you survive? And then I decided that I was going to help other people. That's how I was going to make sense and meaning of what happened. I went back to school and focused on grief and loss and whatever research was being done in those areas. The dissertation for my doctorate was on the sudden death of a sibling during adolescence. It has been a long process, but eventually I found my way. What I always tell people—and I really believe it—is this: My brother's death *defined* my life, but it didn't destroy my life.

"Recently, Robert Neimeyer was a guest on our radio show, and he asked me, 'If your life was a book, what would it look like?' And I said: It would have two chapters. Chapter One would be 'Before My Brother's Death' and Chapter Two would be 'After.'"

CHAPTER 4

Anticipatory Grieving

Ruth's older sister Sharon was several weeks shy of her fortieth birthday when she was told that she had multiple sclerosis, a chronic, degenerative disease of the nervous system. Tall, blond, and graceful, Sharon had been experiencing some disquieting symptoms and behaviors: weakness, loss of coordination, the need to grab a chair, a railing, anything to steady herself. Her vision became impaired. She dropped a platter when serving guests in her home. The diagnosis was devastating. Looking back at the many years when Sharon struggled before finally succumbing to the disease, Ruth now says, "When I heard the news . . . *that's* when I started to mourn."

In the beginning, Sharon just needed a little assistance. For example, she could no longer drive. Ruth would visit her sister's home frequently, trying to help out, to shoulder some of the responsibilities of care that now fell to Sharon's husband and young daughter, Jessica. But the demands of her own life, including two active youngsters, also called upon her. More and more, Ruth found herself watching from the sidelines as Sharon became increasingly dependent on others—especially their parents—to help her get through the day. "I lost the sister I knew years before her actual death," recalls Ruth, now in her late sixties.

Letting go is a process, one that often begins when the person affected by the long-term illness is still alive. It is fairly common for the well siblings to experience what I have come to think of as sequential grieving. As did Ruth, they grieve when they learn of the condition, they grieve as the illness progresses and the patient regresses, they grieve anew when death claims its victim. During the long goodbye, the well sibling will sometimes experience *decathexis*—the gradual weakening of emotional ties, a protective distancing from the ailing sibling.

Ruth now chides herself for having "abandoned" her sister during her later years. Still, her memories of Sharon remain overshadowed by memories of the illness. There is, however, a saving grace to the story. It is the extremely close and loving relationship that exists between Ruth and Jessica, who are more like mother and daughter than aunt and niece. "In being there for my niece," Ruth says, "I feel that I have reconnected with the best part of my sister."

MAKING BARGAINS WITH GOD

Most of the stories in the previous chapters involve men and women who suffered the random tragedy of a sudden and shocking death of a brother or sister. They had no time to prepare for the death, to slowly get used to the idea that life would go on without that sibling, to say goodbye. This chapter focuses on survivors who have lived with the knowledge that their sibling would likely predecease them. I count myself in this group. I remember thinking, when our mother became ill with Alzheimer's disease, *Oh please, God, don't let my sister die before my mother.* The point is, I anticipated that my sister would die. I was just trying to buy some more time with her.

Anyone whose life is linked to a loved one with a long and fatal illness will relate to this concept of bargaining with God. (*Please, God, let my brother who has AIDS respond to the new treatment* or *Please, God, let my sister who has heart disease rally so she can make it to her daughter's wedding.*) Faith can be very helpful. Even people who profess not to believe in a deity are likely to find themselves offering up prayers "to whom it may concern." Though we anticipate the loss of the loved person, we may refuse to accept that death is imminent. In short, we hope against hope.

LIVING IN THE SHADOW OF DYING

"Anticipatory grief does not have to mean premature detachment," writes bereavement specialist Therese A. Rando, Ph.D., in her book, *How to Go On Living When Someone You Love Dies.* "This is the key to healthy anticipatory grief.... In essence, you must recognize and prepare for the future in which you will be without this person physically.

But you can continue to be involved with him in the here-and-now.... We can mourn the future without relinquishing the present."

To understand how this happens, I sought out survivors who lived from early on with the knowledge that their sibling would die, whose role in the family was to be the well sibling, and whose identity was shaped by the love and loss of their childhood companion. I read (and recommend to my readers) Elizabeth DeVita-Raeburn's *The Empty Room*, a moving account of growing up as the younger sister and only sibling of Ted, who suffered from a rare autoimmune disease, causing him to spend eight years living in a plastic bubble where he died at the age of seventeen. I also came upon (and could not put down) *Sixtyfive Roses*, "a sister's memoir" by Heather Summerhayes Cariou, and I set a date to meet with the author.

Heather was six years old when her four-year-old sister Pam ("small, slight, and with a mysterious cough") was diagnosed with cystic fibrosis. "My mom told the two of us together," Heather says. (She pronounces "mom" as "mum," which is how it is said in Canada, where the family lives.) "She also told us there was no cure for it." The doctor had given the child little time to live. "Six weeks, six months," he told the stricken parents. "Maybe if you're lucky and watch her closely you might get six years." Although more recent treatments have successfully increased the expected life span of those who suffer from cystic fibrosis to well into adulthood, in the 1950s, when Pam was diagnosed, few children with the disease lived to attend elementary school. Pam defied those expectations and died at the age of twenty-six. And in all those years, as is often the case in such situations, the illness took and held center stage in the family drama.

I ask Heather: "From the age of six, you knew that your sister was going to die, and you lived with that knowledge—and that fear—for the next twenty-two years. Can you tell me what that was like?"

"It was overpowering, overwhelming," she replies. "As a child, I experienced tremendous fear of mortality. I couldn't believe that Pam was going to die, and by herself, so I promised that I was going to die with her. Then every time she got mortally ill, which she did several times, I became mortally afraid—not just for her but for myself. I used to be afraid that the house would burn down, so I couldn't go to bed at night without having certain things with me—my bedclothes, my doll, my own poetry. I always wrote poetry. As I grew up and matured, I learned that there are things that you think with your head and then there are things that you feel beneath what you know, and sometimes I think that the more primal feelings rule instead of what logic tells you. You are very aware of death."

From the moment of diagnosis, life changed for everyone in the family. In her memoir, Heather writes, "The world of chronic-terminal illness is, in many ways, akin to the world of war," existing as a parallel universe to what might be termed "the real world." In the world of war there were frequent medical crises. Regular routines were thrown into disarray. Hopes rose and plummeted.

Strategizing about how to manage each setback, how to gain some ground became the primary role of the Summerhayes parents. The effort led them to start the Canadian Cystic Fibrosis Foundation, a noteworthy accomplishment but one that Heather viewed, growing up, as another rival for her parents' attention. "It wasn't so much the feeling that I didn't matter," she says, "but of what's more important than a life-and-death struggle. So if somebody teases you at school or you fall off your bike and scrape your knee, it's just not up there on the list of priorities."

What would have helped: "So growing up, what would have helped me is if people would have listened to me more. My parents didn't have a lot of time to listen to me. This is where I feel that our extended family members let us all down. My aunts and uncles . . . Somebody could have taken me for ice cream and asked, 'Tell me how *you* feel.' Everybody was always asking 'How's Pam?' Nobody ever said, 'How are you? How's Heather?' They would ask, 'How are your parents?' Like I wasn't feeling the same things my parents were feeling, only with less ability to deal with them as well."

What did help: "My maternal grandparents were really there for me," Heather says. "I spent a lot of time at their house. And a teacher in seventh grade. She saw me. She understood that I was a poet and supported that. And that gave me an identity outside of being Pam's sister."

Further, Heather was shaken by the deaths of other children. "Because of our involvement with cystic fibrosis," she says, "we lived in a world where other kids died and I started going to funerals. That's when I really lost it." She could not bring herself to be angry at Pam, whom she dearly loved, so she directed her fury against her parents. "I went into an uncontrollable rage that lasted many years."

When people look at stages of grief, of the ways we react to the death of a loved one, **guilt** and **anger** are responses frequently highlighted. For Heather, however, as for others who live with an awareness of death's likelihood, even while the person we love is still alive, the grief journey begins earlier. "The mourning process for my sister did not begin with Pam's death," Heather explains. "I was mourning her through her life. It just changed in quality and intensity after her death.

"In the early stages following her death, I was so angry. I would think: *What are other people doing, walking up and down this street and laughing? Don't they know my sister's dead!!!* You're so mad that the rest of the world is going on. But in time you come to realize that it's the cycle of life. Life goes on.

"I started my book four years after Pam died, and it took me twenty years to complete it. Some memories were so hurtful. A friend of mine said, 'You think that when you finish this book your relationship with your sister will end again, but I'm telling you that it will be even better because the two of you will go out together hand in hand with this story. She'll be with you every step of the way.' He was right.

"I've now lived without Pam as long as I lived with her," Heather says. "As I'm growing older and I have different experiences, this changes my experience of my grief. It changes the moments when I'm overcome with it, it changes how I deal with it. My grief has become like an old friend, and I don't fight it anymore. But then again, it's no longer with me every day. I hear a song on the radio . . . or I'm just walking up the street on a fall morning, and it's windy, and there are the leaves. I see something and I think, *If only Pam could see this.* And then I say to myself: well, she *is* seeing it. I don't know whether I'm seeing the world through Pam's eyes or if she's seeing it through mine."

A personal faith has been helpful: Heather mentions God several times in the interview, so I ask her about her faith. "The moment that Pam died was the moment I really came to believe in God, by whatever name you want to call God," she says. "I believe that there is a power greater than us, but that power is not out on a cloud someplace. I believe that God can express through every human being. It's up to every human being to open themselves up to that expression. When Pam died, it was just so inexplicable to me that she could stop. The body stops, but that energy has to go *somewhere*. Pam still exists . . . even if it's just as a healing force in the universe. That spirit was just too huge and too strong, too sweet. When she was dying and I was holding her hand, I felt it pass from her body. It was there . . . and then it wasn't. So I think it flew and I think I am imbued with some of it." Faith can be a meaningful source of comfort for many mourners.

I ask Heather: "Your sister Pam—and therefore the family—experienced one crisis after another over the years. Did you ever view her death as a relief?"

"Yes," she says. "It was a relief for her, it was a relief for all of us."

"And how did you feel about that sense of relief?"

"Guilty," she responds.

She also says, "Pam and I used to talk about the difference between having a sudden loss or a long loss. We agreed that we got to say what we needed to say to one another. I'm grateful for that."

CHAPTER 5

Death by Suicide

Michelle Linn-Gust's younger sister Denise was eighteen years old when she walked out of her high school, across the faculty parking lot, through the playing fields, and past the industrial park that lined the railroad tracks in her suburban Chicago neighborhood. When a freight train approached, she walked in front of it.

The night before, Denise and Michelle (who was home from college for a brief visit) had sat up on their mom's bed, talking about Denise's plans to attend the University of Chicago in Illinois the following fall. The sisters were used to sharing late-night confidences—they had occupied the same bedroom for ten years before their older brother and sister grew up and moved out. Still, Denise had her private demons, her bad days, causing her to fall behind in her schoolwork, drop out of the band, battle bulimia, to make an earlier attempt at suicide by swallowing two hundred fifty aspirin. In light of past history, Michelle saw the talk of college plans as hopeful. The next morning, she knocked on Denise's door to see if she was getting up for school. "Denise mumbled something I did not understand," says Michelle, "so I went for a run, attended a basketball game I was covering for the college paper, and returned to school. By 10 a.m., my sister was dead."

Michelle received the news at school. And everything changed in her life.

Her role within the family changed. "There was now one less kid to carry on, to get married, to have grandchildren," she says. "I became the baby, the youngest living, and that was very difficult because I was used to having someone after me. When our Christmas cards went out, I was now the last in our family named."

She found herself re-evaluating her values, her friendships, her goals.

Over 30,000 people in the United States die by suicide every year. It is the fourth-leading cause of death for adults between the ages of eighteen and sixty-five. The statistics notwithstanding, survivors often feel very much alone. Further, the grieving process for those left to face the stark reality of the suicide is complicated by a number of issues.

They do *not* talk about the death. Interviews with surviving siblings in all other situations make abundantly clear that what is most beneficial in helping them cope with the loss is "telling the story." In contrast, people whose brother or sister ended their own lives rarely talk about it. The stigma often associated with suicide leads these survivors to keep to themselves or to fudge the actual cause of death. "Such deaths are likely to trigger social awkwardness and embarrassment, preventing bereaved family members from seeking support and reducing the likelihood of others offering it," write Gordon Riches and Pam Dawson in *An Intimate Loneliness: Supporting Bereaved Parents and Siblings.*

I speak with a man in his seventies whose sister met her death forty years earlier by jumping from a roof. "It took me twenty years before I could discuss it with anyone," he says. "If people asked, I would tell them she died of a heart problem." He reaches for a tissue, wipes his eyes. He finds it difficult to speak about his sister's death even now but thanks me at the interview's conclusion. "It has been good to talk about her," he says. "I think of my sister frequently. She had so much potential. You don't forget these things. You never do." Survivors are saddened by thoughts of what might have been.

They do not get a chance to say goodbye. When the brother or sister dies by suicide, as is true for any sudden death, there is no opportunity (as in cases of anticipatory grieving) for survivors to say what is in their hearts. Says Michelle, "One of the most difficult things for me in dealing with my sister's death was that I never told her that I loved her. I've been thinking of that a lot, and I'm sure she knew without my saying it because you can tell by people's actions as well as their words, but I wish I had said it."

Survivors often feel shunned rather than supported. Suicide is an awkward subject. Aware that rumors are rampant in the community, family members tend to pull in their tents and close themselves off from others for a while. (Though suicide can bring a family closer, it can also tear it apart. Rifts are widened, there's more than enough blame to go around.) Meanwhile, even well-meaning friends and acquaintances may not know what to say, what words of solace to offer, and so they distance themselves. Thus, at a time when survivors most need support, they typically find themselves peculiarly alone.

Michelle experienced that detachment when she returned to college following her sister's funeral. "The most frustrating part was that the people I worked with every night at the school paper couldn't be supportive," she says. "A lot of grieving has to do with life experience, but they didn't have that kind of experience. They expected that I would just give it a few weeks and then get back to work. I thought so, too, and believed something had to be wrong with me when I *wasn't* fine and I couldn't go back to work as usual."

In search of information: Knowledge about what to expect when your sibling commits suicide would have been helpful, she says, but twenty years ago such information was hard to come by. "Back then, there wasn't the Internet," she says. "I couldn't just Google 'Sibling Suicide Loss' and come up with all the information that's now available. Today there are survivor support groups, message boards. [Michelle now has her own message board: www.siblingsurvivors.com.] Those who have survived a sibling's suicide are able to connect and communicate via e-mail. There are 384 suicide survivor support groups in the current database of the American Association of Suicidology. Connecting to others in my situation would have been a blessing. I might have realized that my feelings were normal."

The guilt factor: People who lose a brother or sister to suicide deal with unique issues. Though the death may be sudden, there is no random tragedy for them to rue, no drunk driver to blame. Instead, many who are left behind blame themselves, wondering what clues they might have missed, how they might have successfully intervened with a sibling who engaged in self-destructive behaviors like taking drugs or alcohol, whether any action they could have taken might have brought about a different outcome.

"Guilt is a main component of survivor pain," write Ann Smolin and John Guinan in their book, *Healing After the Suicide of a Loved One.* Specifically focusing on the depression that leads many to cross the line between enduring life's burdens and surrendering to them, the authors point out that no one treatment is guaranteed to be best for an individual. "This is very important for survivors who repeatedly blame themselves for not having recognized their loved one's depression and for not getting treatment that would have prevented the suicide," they write, noting that mental health professionals are not always able to successfully treat depression but must sometimes rely on trial and error to see which treatment works for a particular patient. "If highly trained professionals cannot be absolutely sure, the families should not believe they might have been able to prevent the suicide," the authors say.

About anger: For some who are left to mourn, the mystery at the heart of the suicide is not so much *Why did you do it?* as it is *How could you do this?*... quickly followed by *How could you do this to me?* Survivors may feel anger at the deceased, anger at self (I should have seen her more often... I should have phoned... I should have listened), anger at God.

A TALE OF ANGER

Six years ago, when Sean ended his life at age forty, his sister Caitlin was not so much surprised as saddened. Brother and sister had different fathers but grew up in the same house and were close. Five years—no, make that four and a half—separated the two. "Sean would always insist on the technicality," Caitlin explains.

"My brother was sweet, good, a really intelligent person," she goes on, "but there definitely were psychological problems. It's like he was born without any skin—he didn't have buffers between him and the world, and so everything was a different onslaught. He'd been going to a therapist from age eight or nine, and he didn't want to live even then. He felt that life was miserable and that he should be able to end it whenever he wanted to. He was pretty open about it. If you were having a heart-to-heart talk with him, this would come up. And Sean only had heart-to-hearts. He didn't do chitchat. He married at a fairly young age, adopted two children, separated from his wife, and ended up in a bitter custody battle. But then things seemed to get better. Still, he wasn't interested in being happy."

At three o'clock on a Friday afternoon, Caitlin got a call from their mother. "I could hear from her voice that something was wrong. 'Sean,' she said in an anguished tone. Just the one word, 'Sean.' And I knew what had happened.

"Sean was dead.

"He had planned this for a very long time, had released a lethal amount of nitrous oxide into a plastic bag and had breathed it in."

Caitlin flew to be with her mother, leaving her husband and teen-age children at home. "I guess I felt some embarrassment, shame, not wanting to subject the kids to all this. In retrospect, I think that was a mistake. Having my family around would have supported me through a very difficult time." Mostly she felt angry. "I was so mad at Sean for a long time. I was pissed. My mother and I would almost laugh about it. We would say things like 'I am so mad at Sean I could kill him.' Leaving me to deal with the kids, with his ex-wife, it was really a nightmare. How do I feel six years later? I feel that ending his life was my brother's choice and I don't have a right to be sad because this is what he wanted. But I do have a right to be mad because this is not what *I* wanted."

Michelle Linn-Gust expresses a similar sentiment about her sister's resolution. She says, "Some people might feel that Denise wasn't in her right mind when she made the decision to end her life, but I think she really felt she could not go on. That's her choice and she made it." In the next breath, she adds, "But for me, I'm still here and *I* have a life and I have to make the most of it."

The power of the written word: Addressing an early need to keep Denise in her life, Michelle began by writing her sister a letter. "I told her all these things that were happening without her, that some TV shows were ending, that we were eating frozen yogurt, trivial things, because these were the things we used to share day to day. I kept it going for a few months."

Writing a letter to the deceased has helped other grievers. In their book, Smolin and Guinan tell about a woman named Donna who felt both angry at her sister for choosing to die and guilty because she was moving on in her own life. Donna wrote a letter to her sister, telling her everything she was feeling. "Writing this letter was comforting for Donna because it made her feel as if she were still in touch with her sister, even though she was painfully aware that her sister would never read it," the authors write. Donna continued to "communicate" with her sister in this way for many years. "It was her private way of keeping her sister with her in spirit whenever she wanted her to be there."

Michelle also kept a journal (a practice she has engaged in since age seven) and found that writing down her thoughts and reminiscences, mapping her grief journey, was her most useful way of coping. Some of those notes later served as the basis for a paper she wrote in graduate school, which in turn grew into a book, *Do They Have Bad Days in Heaven?* Its subtitle: *Surviving the Suicide Loss of a Sibling.*

She reached out to the American Association of Suicidology, was asked to speak at the association's conference, edits its newsletter,

Surviving Suicide, and is one of the cochairs for the International Association for Suicide Prevention.

I say to her: "People now contact you for the kind of support you wish had been available to you after Denise died. What are the questions that you hear most often?"

She answers, "They ask: Am I going to survive this? How did you survive this? They are looking for some hope."

"And you say . . . ?"

"I let people know. I remember being there. I remember what it was like to live one minute at a time, one hour at a time. That's okay. And I try to let them know there are things that they can do to remember the person . . . because you can't take all those years with that person away. Whether it's writing or talking about the person. Or making a disc of their favorite songs. Or going to the cemetery and placing something on the grave. Or participating in a community walk. Or getting in touch with the Suicide Prevention Action Network and contributing to the Faces of Suicide Quilt. They don't have to do this alone."

Joining a support group helps: "I have three brothers," says Rick Mogil when asked to describe his family. *I have three brothers* . . . even though Ed, third from the top in this four-boy family, has been dead for five years. Rick, sixty-one, is the oldest son. Asked to describe Ed, he paints a portrait of someone about whom he cared deeply but could not save from a lifelong addiction.

"I was eight years old when Ed was born," he says. "He and I both suffered from asthma and allergies, which created a special bond between us. From early on, however, Ed was involved with alcohol and drugs. As a child, he would finish off the residue of drinks from party glasses. At nine, he drank himself drunk at the family seder. He was dealing drugs in high school. He was depressed.

"He was also a talented artist. He drew some very revealing pictures about suicide and about how he felt. I don't think he showed them to any of his teachers, because if they had seen them—especially the one that shows a skeleton hanging from a tree—they probably would have said he needs to be in some kind of therapy. He made several suicide attempts and spent some time in rehab. He married, found work running a hatchery, did well at it, but could not recognize his worth."

On a day late in January 2003, Ed left his home and was reported missing. Three days later, there came a call. He'd been found in a hotel room, dead of a self-inflicted gunshot wound. He was forty-eight years old—part of a new and troubling trend. A five-year analysis of the nation's death rates released by the federal Centers for Disease Control and Prevention reports that the suicide rate among 45-to-54-year-olds increased nearly 20 percent from 1999 to 2004, the last year for which figures are available. The reason for this increase, however, is still not understood.

Rick was devastated by what Ed had done.

Finding a suicide-specific support group: "One of my cousins who came to the memorial service gave me some information about Al-Anon and suggested I contact them," he says. "It took about two weeks before I acted on it. At my first meeting I shared, which is what they do, and I found it interesting that I did that because I'm someone who would never share my feelings with anybody, including my wife. I always kept things in. This was the first time I actually talked in front of a group of about forty people who were complete strangers to me. After the meeting, three or four of them approached me, saying that they, too, had lost a sibling to suicide, and that they understood what I was going through. One of them gave me a number for a survivors program at Didi Hirsch Community Mental Health Center here in California and she said, 'You need to call these people.' I hesitated. She said, 'I will call the director and I will have her call you, and you go from there.'"

In the meantime, Rick consulted a bereavement specialist, which didn't work out. "She made statements that just weren't appropriate, like 'Suicide is totally a selfish act,'" he says. "I stopped going after three or four sessions and went only to Al-Anon meetings until I got into a Survivors After Suicide program at Didi Hirsch, and I realized that I had come to where I needed to be."

Rick's point is well taken. People may advise you to see a bereavement specialist, they may recommend joining a support group—either or both can be useful in helping one cope with suicide's consequences—but not every counselor nor every program is right for every person. Trust your instincts. If the person or place is not right for you, don't give up. Instead, seek a different recommendation.

Rick went through the program, eight Saturdays in a row, an hour and a half each session, led by a facilitator who is a therapist trained in suicide bereavement issues, and cofacilitated by one or two volunteer survivors. "I was the only one with a sibling loss," he says. "Everybody else in the group was there because of having lost a spouse, a child, there may have been one who lost a parent. After the first two sessions, I started thinking, *My God, what am I doing here? There are parents who've lost their children, while I've only lost my brother. It doesn't measure up.* After the fourth session I realized it doesn't matter who you lost. The fact is that you've lost somebody to suicide and it's totally different than any other kind of loss." (For more on the subject of what to look for in a support group, see Chapter 8.)

Following death, finding a way of life: Finding ways to make sense of the loss of a loved one motivates some survivors to take up work in the area of counseling, to reach out to others. This has been the case for Michelle; it is true in Rick's life as well; it is behind the efforts of Alison, whom we meet later in this chapter.

At the end of the eight-week support program, Rick was asked if he wanted to train to become a cofacilitator. If he could help others, he thought, that might give some meaning to the senselessness of Ed's death. He took the training and then volunteered at the center for three years before coming on board full time as coordinator for the Survivors After Suicide Response Team—men and women who go out to the scene of a suicide within minutes or hours of its happening to help families through that initial bereavement.

"To my mind," he says, "the loss of a sibling is the loss of our present, past, and future. If it's a younger sibling, that's the one who is supposed to help bury *you*, and you're burying him, before your parents. When I speak to siblings, I make that point—that they're busy taking care of their parents, that they're taking care of the spouse and children of the deceased, and that they need also to take care of themselves. And there are people that can help them. Our number is 877-727-4747. Any place that has a survivors group, that's the place to go."

"You're in Southern California," I say. "Suppose someone needs help in Vermont."

"Then they should phone 800-273-TALK—the National Suicide Hotline—to be directed to a center nearest them."

In this day of technology, Rick has also created a Web site—a means that many survivors use to commemorate the life of the deceased. His is www.lifeaftersuicide.org. It shows photos of the four brothers, displays Ed's drawings, directs people to sites where they can find more information about surviving a suicide.

"What helped me most was someone saying something to me—my cousin telling me about Al-Anon," he says. "I felt that I was at the end of my rope. I didn't know what to do. Someone handed me a lifeline. And I took it."

From the darkness comes a light: Alison Malmon was eighteen and a freshman at the University of Pennsylvania in March 2000 when her brother and only sibling, Brian, twenty-two, took his life . . . and forever changed hers.

"My brother and I were very close," she says. "Our parents separated when I was eight and Brian was twelve, and at that point—going back and forth to our dad's house—we really bonded. It was very important, having a brother with me. We even looked like one another—people often mistook us for twins and many spoke of us as a couple: Alison-and-Brian. The give-and-take between us was incredible. His strengths (he was the history and English person) were my weaknesses and my strengths (math, science) were his weaknesses, so we never competed with one another, as siblings often do."

Instead, Alison applauded Brian's considerable achievements. At New York's Columbia College, he was president of an a capella group named Uptown Local, was sports editor of *Spectator*, the school newspaper, and star of the Varsity Show, while still maintaining a high grade point average. Friends (of whom he had many) spoke about his sharp wit, dry humor, energy, and intelligence. What neither friends nor family knew, however (because Brian guarded his secret so carefully), was that he did all of this while suffering from schizoaffective disorder, a combination of schizophrenia and a mood disorder such as depression. His was a constant struggle to suppress the voices that had begun visiting him in February of his freshman year.

"He did not want anybody to know that something was different with him because he was embarrassed by it and he thought it was his fault," says Alison. Three years into his illness, Brian took a leave of absence from school and came home to Potomac, Maryland. It was the first time the family learned of his illness.

"We come from a family that is very supportive and knows about feelings and about behavioral issues, and it still boggles my mind how Brian kept it so quiet for so long," says Alison. Once home, he went for treatment, which included medicine and intensive therapy. On March 24, 2000, eighteen months after leaving school, Brian ended his struggle with a self-inflicted gunshot wound. Alison, sister and soul mate, was a freshman at the University of Pennsylvania when she heard the news. That's when her own struggle to understand and accept the loss of her big brother began.

Replacing fear with knowledge: "I dove into research on the subject because I didn't know what else to do with myself," says the self-possessed young woman. "What I found was that Brian's first experiencing symptoms during his freshman year was *not* unique, that mental health disorders typically first present during the high school and college years, and I got really scared. Since Brian and I were such similar people, I realized that had I started experiencing what he did—had I started hearing voices, had I been depressed—I, too, would have kept it quiet. I would never have told my family. I wouldn't have wanted to tell my friends. And even if I had, my friends wouldn't have known what to say to me because there was never a dialogue around these issues."

Alison reached out to a grief and loss support group on her campus. "It was for students who had lost somebody, although I was the only one who had lost a sibling," she says. "Further, I was the only person who had lost someone to suicide." Although she found the group a great support ("because it helped me feel that I wasn't alone"), Alison was stirred by Brian's death to address the stigma attached to the mental illness that had brought it about, that had kept her brother from seeking necessary help for the first three years of the illness, instead giving in to the despair that makes one see death as the only way out.

"In addition to my fear, there was also a growing realization that there probably were people on my campus who were going through what Brian had experienced at his school," she tells me. The statistics support her hypothesis. According to the Suicide Prevention Resource Center, suicide is the second-leading cause of death among college students. Alison went to the counseling center at her school and said, "I want to do something on campus. I want to make mental health issues as widely discussed as physical issues and to let young people know that they are not alone. I want the group to be student led, to encourage students to tell their own stories, to educate other students to the signs and symptoms of the different mental health disorders and the resources that exist for seeking help."

Three people came to the first meeting of what eventually became Active Minds, the nonprofit organization Alison founded and now serves as executive director. Five years later, there are 145 chapters at colleges and universities across the country, with an expectation that there'll be 300 chapters by the year 2010.

"I get letters from people periodically, expressing gratitude," says Alison. "Some have told us that becoming part of Active Minds has saved their lives." She wishes that there had been such an organization to support Brian. Where once there was deception and darkness, she strives for openness and light. "This isn't just about Brian and me," says the surviving sister. "It's about destigmatizing mental illness. We want to have students feel free to get help and not have to hide their illness or struggle alone with their demons."

What helps Alison deal with her grief is the work that she does every day. In memory of a much-loved brother who took his own life, she has thrown out a lifeline to save others.

Plea

Forgive me for the promises I've broken.
I wanted to commemorate your life,
to say what you were like—funny, soft-spoken—
to tell stories about you, to describe your laugh,
but I seem to have written only of your death.
Forgive me, I've placed your photos on my shelf.
I look into your eyes in disbelief.
Can I forgive you for killing yourself?

Forgive me for not calling you more often,
especially those last weeks of your life.
Forgive the silences, the words not spoken,
forgive these words too late to give relief,
the tears I've shed and haven't shed in grief.
Forgive me for always thinking of myself
and for not seeing that you needed help—
and I will forgive you for killing yourself.

I'd like to believe the words that were spoken
at your memorial: that you are safe
in heaven. But we are here, heartbroken.
Even if there is an afterlife,
it's closed to the living, whatever our belief.
No one can forgive me but myself,
I see that now. You can't lighten my grief.
But I can forgive you for killing yourself.

Andy, you who were unable to ask for help,
"Beloved Son, Brother, and Uncle" (your epitaph),
if you can hear me beyond the bounds of death:
I forgive you for killing yourself.

—Jeffrey Harrison, whose brother Andy killed
himself in November 2002, at age forty-seven.

CHAPTER 6

9/11—Dealing with a Public Death

My sister died on September 5, 2001, and was buried on September 7. In keeping with Jewish tradition, I was sitting *shiva* (a seven-day period of mourning, following the funeral, in which members of the immediate family are visited at home by the community, memorial prayers are recited, the life of the deceased is recalled) when I got a call from my husband who was in downtown Manhattan. "Something's happened. Turn on the television," he said.

9/11 happened.

Suddenly my private mourning was subsumed by the global tragedy: thousands of people killed in an unforeseen and unprecedented act of terrorism. How could I speak about my sister when so many people lost loved ones so swiftly and senselessly?

A similar concern was expressed by my friend Joel, whose wife was among those who died at the World Trade Center that day. "How do I deal with a private loss—the death of my wife—in the midst of so much tragedy?" Joel asked when we met in the days and weeks after the event.

I could not answer, and so we hugged in silent sadness.

But I continued to ponder the question of death in the public eye. Year after year when I would see the televised tributes to the victims of 9/11, when I would watch transfixed as family members rose to solemnly read the names of those who perished, I would wonder how the mourners were managing, what sources of emotional support they'd been able to call upon, what life for them was like away from the cameras.

I knew it couldn't be easy.

"Deaths caused by murder or mass tragedy, such as 9/11, mining disasters, or plane crashes cannot be grieved in private," says P. Gill White in her book, *Sibling Grief*. "They usually involve additional factors, such as legal factors that delay the resolution of grief. Wherever the mourners go, people are talking about the event that killed their sibling. Attention from the media adds stress to already overstressed survivors."

The news coverage continues. As the 9/11 disaster neared its sixth anniversary, an article in my morning paper reported controversy surrounding the upcoming commemoration, which was to include a public ceremony and reading of the names of the deceased. According to the story, some people saw this as excessive. Expressing the belief that enough is enough, one woman was quoted as saying, "I may sound callous, but doesn't grieving have a shelf life?"

"I hear statements like this all the time," says grief specialist Heidi Horsley, who was enlisted to work with families of those who lost their lives on that fateful day. One group she's involved with has been meeting for six years. Says Horsley, "Some people thought the group should be dismantled, and they said to me, 'Heidi, how long should this go on?' And I said, 'As long as the participants want it to.' And they said, 'Well, what if it's thirty years?' And I said, 'Then it's thirty years.' I don't like it when the world puts time frames on our grief and they feel that people should be at a certain place at a certain time. Grieving is very individual."

The public nature of the death is further underscored by the fact that those who died that day are often referred to as a group—the 9/11 victims—and their survivors as 9/11 families: not as John's brother or Mary's sister. "The families I work with say that all the time," says Horsley. "'This wasn't about 9/11,' they say. 'This was about Johnnie or Frankie or Marylou. This is not about a public event; it's about my own personal loss. I'm missing this person in my life.'"

In mourning the individual victim, however, John's brother or Marylou's sister is likely to have turned to fellow grievers for much-needed support. As a general experience, the loss of a loved one is swiftly followed by a funeral or memorial service, burial or cremation—acts that signal the beginning of a period of mourning. With most of the 9/11 families, however, there are no identifiable remains of the one who died, there was no official burial or scattering of ashes. "Their bereavement is further complicated by the fact that they were denied a formalized path to travel in the early days and weeks after the loss," says Simcha Weintraub, rabbinic director of the National Center for Jewish Healing, based in New York.

For many survivors, therefore, allying themselves with the larger group *is* a way of coping.

Like Heidi Horsley, Rabbi Weintraub has been working with family members of those who perished on 9/11. He tells of recently receiving a call from out of town. "The caller, a woman who had lost a brother on 9/11, had heard that our post-9/11 group was still meeting, and she asked, very politely, if they would mind if she visited," he says. "She came by and the members loved her and she them, and they welcomed her to join them if she could make it to New York for the monthly meetings. My heart goes out to this woman who for six and a half years found no sibling support."

Two years ago, Rabbi Weintraub led his 9/11 group on a healing trip to Israel. "The purpose was to spend two weeks, mostly with Israelis and Palestinians who had lost family members to violence and terror," he says. "It was a powerful meeting." Some days into the trip, he asked the 9/11 surviving family members what was different between their experience and those of the Israelis and Palestinians whom they met. "Almost to a person," he reports, "they said, 'They have a narrative and we don't.' Of course, all the different Israelis and the different Palestinians had very different narratives: self-determination . . . or creating a homeland . . . or love of Jerusalem . . . or on and on. But the 9/11 mourners felt that their loved ones went off to work one morning and never came home, and for two-thirds of them no body parts were ever found. And so they not only lack an immediate, individual, and personal narrative but the ability to place what happened in some bigger story. Survivors of trauma need some way to think of their story."

Perhaps that is one reason for the continued participation by 9/11 survivors in ceremonies commemorating the event. It may help make sense of it all. For them, the private anguish and the public act collide.

IN MEMORIAM: JEANETTE LAFOND-MENICHINO

The person missing in Anita Korsonsky's life is Jeanette LaFond-Menichino, her younger sister, who was forty-nine at the time she was killed in the terrorist attack. (Reflecting the violent nature of what happened, Anita never says her sister died, always speaks of "the time when my sister was killed.") In the newspaper article that appeared around the time of the sixth anniversary, Anita spoke against scaling back the memorial tributes. "To say six years is enough, it's not," she was quoted as saying. "I don't know what's enough."

That the pain is enduring is corroborated by a longitudinal study being conducted at Columbia University that looks at loss over time. Families in the study were first seen eleven months after 9/11 and have been followed every year since then. An interesting finding, says Heidi Horsley who is involved in the study, is that "six years was a breakthrough for widows; they really were in a healing place and had forged new identities as single women. In contrast, the parents and siblings felt that they could not move forward like that because they could never replace their child or their sibling."

I speak with Anita to learn what those six years have been like for her and where she is today.

Some events are distinct in our memory—we recall exactly where we were and what we were doing at the time they occurred. 9/11 is one of those events, and here is what Anita remembers.

"It was early, I was at my job as an editor at a New Jersey-based publishing firm, and I decided to check in with my sister, who worked as an assistant vice president at an insurance company on the ninety-fourth floor of the World Trade Center in tower number one. She would always give me a report on the view: sometimes it would be cloudy; sometimes sunny and beautiful, sometimes it would rain below the ninety-fourth floor while the sky was clear above. She'd been out in the rain the night before, and I thought I'd see how she was. It was about twenty to nine and the line was busy. I was still holding on to the receiver when a friend in the next cubicle came in and said, 'Oh my God, I just heard on the radio that a plane hit one of the World Trade Center towers.'

"My first thought was that a plane hit the towers the way a plane had once hit the Empire State Building, that it was an accident. Everybody got their computers up—they already had pictures of the first tower—and I could see where the plane hit. I knew at that moment that my sister was dead."

Anita tried to reach her husband and parents, she tried to reach Jeanette's husband, but the lines were tied up. "I don't remember when I finally spoke with my mother," she says. Anita does recall coming home . . . the phone ringing . . . cousins calling, friends, and relatives . . .

"I remember this so vividly," she says. "I was looking out the window around four o'clock in the afternoon, and it was such a beautiful day, the trees in my backyard were beautiful, and I remember looking up at the sky and it was all blue, and I remember saying, 'Jeanette, where are you?' And I thought, *She's with God. She's in heaven. I don't have to worry about her. She's safe.* You have to believe in God or something like that to deal with something like this."

The sisters had been close. "Growing up, we had fights and arguments as sisters do—I'd sometimes complain about having to drag my little sister around—but basically we got along well," Anita says. "We grew closer as we got older. With a sister you don't always think about your relationship. She's a part of your life. She's just always there." Until she was not there. And Anita found herself struggling to make sense of her sister's public, traumatic demise.

What helped: Spreading the message of love. "One of the things that helped me was to write an article about her that appeared in our company newsletter," Anita says. "My message was that, with people you love—but especially with a sibling—how precious that relationship is, how you don't know when anything is going to end. If you keep a good relationship with the people you love in your life, call them, say I love you, make sure the last conversation you have with them is not an argument or a fight. . . . This is so important because you never know when someone is going to be taken away from you. After I wrote that, people would come up to me and say, 'I thought about what you said, and I just phoned my sister. I hadn't spoken to her for six months.' And I would think, *You haven't talked to your sister for six months?* I don't understand how there could be that dynamic in so important a relationship. If I could help one other person to fix their relationship with a loved one or just understand how fleeting life can be . . . It brings a shaft of light, I guess I could say happiness, to some terrible tragedy."

Dealing with disturbing dreams: Ten months after 9/11, Anita's father died of natural causes, and the shrinking of her family, as well as the need to adjust to new roles, led her to enter therapy. Not only had Anita become an only child with sole responsibility to relate to her remaining parent, but, she says, "On the day Jeanette died, my life as a sister ended. I had to fashion a new life for myself as a person who *had* a sister but who no longer has that relationship as a living entity. It's as if both our lives, as sisters, ended on 9/11. And as she began a new life in the afterlife, I also began a new life here on earth. On the outside I was fine, but on the inside . . . "

She struggled with unsettling memories. "There was another sister, Marie, who was born when I was two," Anita explains. "She had spina bifida and only lived two weeks. Jeanette was born two years later, and she was incredibly precious to my mother. She had little blue eyes and blond hair. She was adorable. And I think, during my childhood, that I resented that a little. Those thoughts kept coming back to me. The therapist told me that those were my thoughts when I was growing up; it was okay to have them. They didn't reflect on my later relationship with my sister.

"I was also having disturbing dreams. In one, Jeanette was on a street corner and she was walking a little bit ahead of me. She would turn a corner, and I would try to catch up with her, but by the time I reached her corner she had turned another corner, so that I couldn't get to her. And then there was another dream of us being on a staircase and it was the same thing. I knew she was ahead of me but I couldn't see her. I'm pretty sure I understood what that meant. I was trying to find her in my life again. And the dream was telling me: You're not going to find her. She isn't there." (See Chapter 11 for more about the role of dreams.)

Asleep or awake, Anita is immersed in reminders of her lost sibling.

Public reminders: "The 9/11 loss is *not* the same as any other," says Heidi Horsley. "It is not, because the families have constant reminders. They go into the supermarket and on the front page of a magazine there's something about 9/11. They don't have control over when they're going to get barraged by these memories. That's a good thing and a bad thing for them. The good news is that they feel like their loved ones will never be forgotten. But the bad news is that they get inundated at times when they don't want to have memories."

"My sister is in my thoughts all the time," Anita says. "I often compare her death to my father's because they happened so close to one another. I do think of my father occasionally but not every day because he died when he was eighty-two. It wasn't so unusual and he was ill. With my sister, I think of her every day because I miss her and because a day doesn't go by that something will come up having to do with September eleventh. If you live in the New York area, it's around all the time. For example, the other day I was in a store, Linens 'n Things, and I walked past the area where they have pictures, and there was a picture of the New York skyline—the older skyline with the World Trade Center towers. So maybe that afternoon I wasn't thinking about my sister, but there I am buying towels and they have this painting and I'm right back there.... I am forever branded as the family member of a 9/11 victim. Even if I am reminded of pleasant memories of our childhood and adult life, I must always end it with her death. Because of its being so public, I want people to remember the people who were there at the time, and what it meant to everyone else to have this happen. And why it happened. It's very important to me."

IN MEMORIAM: STEPHEN SILLER

Stephen Siller, a thirty-five-year-old fireman, was off duty and returning home when he heard on his scanner that the World Trade Center was hit. He turned his car back toward the scene. When he was barred from driving through the Brooklyn Battery Tunnel, he strapped on his gear, weighing about seventy-five pounds, and raced through the tunnel to the towers. It is thought that he was trying to find his company—Squad 1, Park Slope, Brooklyn. He was not seen again.

September 11, 2001, started out as an ordinary day in the Siller household on Staten Island, New York. The three older brothers were waiting for their kid brother Stephen to show up so they could play golf. "It was a great day, a perfect day, no wind," recalls Russell Siller, sixty-two, the family's firstborn. "I'd bought doughnuts for Stephen's five kids and I was at his house when he phoned his wife, Sally. 'Tell the boys I'll be late,' he said. So I went over to my brother Frank's house, just a few minutes away, and we heard that a plane had hit the towers.... Then we heard that another plane hit.... And that was it.

"Then things shifted. It was back to Sally's house. And then waiting... waiting... a couple of days... We'd go back and forth between Frank and Sally's house. The story is similar for all 9/11 families. At a certain point the family realized that the person wasn't coming home. So we had our memorial service on October third. Stephen's remains weren't found then; they haven't been found now. It's an odd thing to have a funeral and a casket without a body.... We never got to play that golf game and we're still waiting for Stephen."

In a tight-knit, Irish Catholic family of seven children, Russell (the oldest) and Stephen (twenty-four years his junior) had a particular bond. Orphaned at the age of ten, Stephen was twelve when he came to live with Russell, a teacher, and his wife Jacqueline, at their home in Rockville Centre, New York. "Stephen was my kid—he was like six kids," Russell says. "He was a force of nature. He rejuvenated me.

When he came to our house everything changed big time because he had all this energy. For example, we come from a very athletic family, and he and I would play one-on-one basketball because I didn't know what else to do with him. I didn't have any kids. I can't tell you how many games of basketball we played. And my wife was a very good counterbalance. Quiet, spiritual, like my mother. My role in his life? When our parents were alive, I was a brother; when he came to live with me, I took on a more fatherly role, but when he went back to Staten Island and became a fireman, I was a brother again. We all miss Stephen in our own ways, but I will tell you, for me to have lost him, personally, was to have lost my soul mate. The earth had been removed from under my feet. Dark, dark, everything was dark. It was horrible.

"I'll tell you about an incident, however. I was sitting at home writing a eulogy for Stephen, for the memorial service, and I kept balling up pieces of paper and flinging them against the wall, cursing. It was not my modus operandi, but I was a little bit out of control, and I screamed, *He had a shitty life*, and I got up and slammed out the back door. It's pitch dark outside—no moon, nothing—and I'm walking down the street, and out of nowhere comes a beach ball shooting towards me, which is something Stephen would do. He was always chipping golf balls, throwing balls, and I went to pick up the ball and a gust of wind blew the ball toward a big intersection. Now I'm racing after this ball as if it were a person, and I picked it up, and I was fine. There was no explanation for a ball to be shooting up out of a parking lot at that moment. None. If Stephen didn't do it, then all the planets were lined up right. That did it. I never hit that darkness again."

Finding support among fellow sufferers: "But I still was troubled," Russell says. "I'm not the kind to seek support. My family isn't. I don't know anybody of the family who went into therapy or anything. In any case, I knew I was overmatched and needed help because this was a public death and everywhere I turned there were 9/11 people and it was horrible. A friend told me about programs for family survivors being run by South Nassau Hospital. I started going to the support group for siblings."

Just as people who lost someone to suicide do best in a group unique to their situation, so too have the 9/11 families required special handling. "When I first came to a meeting (I didn't go right away; it was around Christmas time), there were tissue boxes in front of everybody, and I was so much in denial I thought it was some Buddhist ceremony,"

Russell says. "I didn't even know if I would stay. What was common to us all was total disbelief that such a thing could happen. Our grief was so profound and we were so angry. Every loss is different, but the odds against this kind of death were so long, the attack itself was so outrageous. We bonded in our misery.

"Then I came to know these people and I've watched them grow and watched them work out problems—difficulties with spouses, with in-laws, with the parents, and I realized where I was on the plane of things. I mean, there were discussions at times about who it was worse for: the parents, the spouse, siblings. It provided some interesting meetings, to say the least. I became dear friends with many of them. I will always know them and they will always know me, and for all of us there will always be September 11th. And September 12th. That will never change."

Keeping Stephen's memory alive is a constant focus: "In a sense, I had two support groups," Russell says. "One in Rockville Centre, run by a professional. And I had my own sibling support group, with my family. We got together early on and decided that there was no way we were going to let Stephen go, because he was the glue in our family. We would form a foundation in his memory to benefit children who had lost parents, and we did: the Stephen Siller, FDNY [Fire Department of New York] "Let Us Do Good" Children's Foundation. We were thinking of having a race in Staten Island, and we wondered: What are the odds that we could produce something like that? So we had a meeting with the Department of Transportation and we told Stephen's story: how he was orphaned, how he had five kids, how he did not need to go through the tunnel that day, how much he loved Sally and the kids—no one I know enjoyed fatherhood more. The man whom we met with had tears in his eyes, and he said, 'You'll get your run.' That was the beginning of what became the annual 5K Stephen Siller Tunnel to Towers Run, which retraces the steps my brother took from Brooklyn through the tunnel to the World Trade Center on the last day of his life.

"The first year there were 3,000 people on the run," Russell says. "In 2007, there were 20,000 participants—not all runners, but a lot of runners come with their families. They sign an application and contribute money and then go to the other side of the tunnel, near Ground Zero, where we have food donated by restaurants throughout the city, clowns, face painters. We throw this like it's a party, and that's how

Stephen would have wanted it. We've raised a lot of money for burn centers, for the New York Foundling Hospital, for other charities that benefit children.

"Stephen is gone," says his big brother. "The family pulling together . . . doing good in his name and his memory . . . that's what helps us live with that."

CHAPTER 7

Losing a Twin

It is evident to even a casual observer of the double-stroller explosion that the number of twin and other multiple births has climbed at an unprecedented pace in recent years. In the United States, the incidence of twins increased by over 65 percent between 1980 and 2002. As a result, one sees greater interest generally in the twin experience—in what it is like to be a twin and what it's like to lose a twin. More people find themselves struggling with the pain of that loss. Forty-six twins were among the 3,000 victims of 9/11, for example. Following that tragic day, a weekly support group was formed exclusively for survivors who lost their twins in the attacks, recognizing both the unique relationship enjoyed by twins in life and the uncommon despair they encounter when they are separated by death.

It is that survivor experience—of what it's like to live in a world bereft of one's twin—that we look at here.

The twin relationship is intense: "From before birth, I mean in utero, we have this bond with someone—it's like being in a perfect marriage," says Linda Pountney, who entered this world fifty-six years ago as an identical twin. "You go through life and you bounce everything off your twin. Sometimes twins don't even have as close a relationship with their mother, for example. A lot of our needs are met by our twin.

"You kind of face the world as a 'we,'" she says. "My sister Paula and I were like one entity. People referred to us as 'the twins.' Only a couple of friends knew which one was which." There was also an older brother, Peter. When the sisters were twenty-one, Paula fell to her death in a small plane that plummeted to the ocean off the coast of

Florida. Her body washed ashore four days later. And Linda became an I. "My identity, in large part, was as part of a twinship," she says. "When that's taken away, as twins we don't know how to fit into the singleton world."

Identity issues are particularly difficult for surviving twins to resolve, agrees Nancy Segal, Ph.D., director of the Twins Study Center at California State University, Fullerton. As we saw in previous chapters, many siblings grapple with this issue of "I used to be a brother" or "I used to be a sister" once their sibling dies. But, says Segal, "Twins don't react that way. Years after the death, they still introduce themselves as twins."

After her book, *Entwined Lives: Twins and What They Tell Us about Human Behavior*, was published, Segal started hearing from many people who had lost a twin. "I was impressed with the level of grief they were describing," she tells me. So she conducted a survey that looked at twin grief. "What I found was, one, when you lose a twin (identical or fraternal) it actually is a more severe grief experience than when you lose any other relative," she says. Her studies showed that even those twins who were reared apart and reunited later in life still mourned when the twin died. "The loss of a twin seemed to rank as high as the loss of a spouse among those few twins who had lost a spouse as well," she says. "It didn't surprise me because I'd heard that anecdotally, but what it did was affirm in a rather unique and provocative way just how important the twin relationship is.

"The other thing I learned," she says, "was that for identical twins the loss is more severe than for fraternal twins."

That's very likely because (as studies show) identical twins share closer social bonds than fraternal twins. And because—the reason seems obvious—they look so much alike. "Whenever I look in the mirror, I see my twin," says a woman whose twin sister died five years earlier. "And when people look at me, they see her, too," she adds. "Friends and family members will slip up and call me by her name. I am a living reminder of her life."

Delayed grief: Linda Pountney buried her feelings along with her sister's body—or so it seemed at the time. "I did not go through much of my grief process in the first twenty years after my sister died," she says. "I was not capable to absorb the full magnitude of what it meant to me emotionally. Also, I felt that I didn't need to grieve. I carried my twin with me. She was just a part of me." In that time, Linda married, remarried, was twice divorced, bore two sons. "I think I stayed in my first marriage longer than I should have," she says. "Being a twin, you crave that close relationship." I hear this from other twins as well—they speak of a desire for closeness that they experienced with their twin and of feeling frustration when their efforts at similarly bonding with others fall short of their expectations.

Multiple tragedies followed for Linda. Her older brother Peter was killed in a car crash when he was thirty-four, later her mother and father died. "The grief brought on some real lethargic, heavy feelings in my body. I had a hard time differentiating who I was grieving for."

A year of critical grieving: "At that point, I put myself in therapy, went religiously every week, and realized that there was this huge amount of grief for my twin that had not been addressed. There was no choice; I needed to deal with Paula's loss. I read books on twins, books on grief. And I learned about an organization called Twinless Twins, made up of bereaved twins. I was no longer alone." Linda is now vice president of the international organization.

About Twinless Twins: The story of the founding of Twinless Twins, an international support group that has as its mission "to provide a safe and compassionate community for twinless twins to experience healing and understanding," has become legend. Raymond and Robert Brandt, the third and fourth children in a family that grew to include eleven children, were identical twins. In this large family, their twinness was a distinction that they welcomed. The boys did everything together. The summer they were twenty, they even took a job working as electric linemen for the same company to earn tuition for school. On July 5, 1949, Robert was electrocuted at work and died.

Raymond grew older, earned a doctorate in human engineering, married twice, had four sons . . . and continued to mourn his twin's passing. In 1985, Raymond attended a meeting of the International Twins Association and began seeing double. Everywhere he looked there were twins, and he was alone. "I *used* to be a twin," he told people whom he met at the meeting, explaining his solo presence at the event. He was warmly welcomed. "Once a twin, always a twin," they responded. That became not just his philosophy but the guiding philosophy of the organization Raymond Brandt went on to found. He died in 2001 but would be pleased to see the growth of Twinless Twins, not just in the United States (the main office is in Ypsilanti, Michigan) but in Canada, Australia, and the United Kingdom. Bereaved twins can reach one another through its Web site (www.twinlesstwins.org), at chapter meetings, or at the annual conference.

Studies show that the loss of a twin at a very young age is also profound and enduring. Indeed, there are co-twins who say they feel the pain of loss even though they barely knew their twin. "It is a sense of feeling incomplete," I'm told by a forty-year-old whose twin died in infancy. They may also be experiencing a longing and regret for what might have been.

"I think twins feel closer to other twins than they do to family members," says Nancy Segal, reflecting on the organization's success in helping twins deal with their grief, whether the loss of a twin occurs at birth or at any time along life's spectrum. Raymond Brandt, you will recall, had nine non-twin siblings but turned for comfort to others who had experienced the intimacy of twinship. The support group is about finding people who understand. It's about helping twins deal with the issue of survivor guilt. ("We came into this world together and we were supposed to leave the world together," says a surviving twin.) It's about teaching twins how to live without their other halves.

Putting feelings into words helps: At a meeting of Twinless Twins, Linda met Brandt, who encouraged her to put her feelings into words. Telling the story, writing it down are ways to support the healing process. Linda found it helpful. "I would keep a log at my bedside," she says. "So many things came up, things that I had blocked out. All of these memories of who Paula and I were together . . . It was not filled with only wonderful stuff. I dug down into the nature of who we were as sisters and as friends. I woke up one night thinking, *Did Paula set the limits for who I was?* I never had that identity issue with my brother because we weren't so entwined. With twins, there's usually a leader and a follower. And in childhood, she was definitely the leader. So I wrote that in my log and then I explored it. And I realized that I wasn't Paula, I wasn't just a twin, that there was a *me.*"

Scrapbooking to heal: "I also made a huge scrapbook about Paula and me, and it became vital to my recovery. Included were Paula's letters, achievements, even a lock of her hair. I marveled at pictures of the two of us. I remembered Paula in ways I had forgotten. In doing a scrapbook, you go through photos, jot down memories. And you take it out on special occasions, like the person's birthday or anniversary. People who lose their twins have a difficult time with birthdays, as they were always celebrated together. You may want to write a letter or note on that day and place it in the book."

Keeping alive the memories of those we have lost is a step forward, not backward, mourners find. "After my younger son was born, I wanted to share my family with him, but I didn't know how to do that," says Linda. "I consulted a grief counselor. She encouraged me to put pictures out, to talk about my family when I needed to, to rejoice in their life. She said, 'Your relationship to these people doesn't end.'

"Unfortunately, a lot of the world is uncomfortable with that," Linda says. "I'm not."

CHAPTER 8

The Bereavement Support Group

"What helped you cope with your grief?"

I'm not surprised to hear survivors respond: finding Al-Anon, joining The Compassionate Friends, locating a Survivors After Suicide meeting, learning about a program for people who lost their siblings on 9/11, discovering Twinless Twins.

I'm not surprised because, in a different context, I have been both a member and a leader of support groups, and I have seen how effective a successful group can be. I believe in the value of support groups. I have witnessed the validation and understanding that people encounter when they enter a room and find many there who have had similar experiences and share some of the same feelings. I have felt the relief that comes with knowing that in this safe environment one can speak openly and without censure of one's situation and one's sorrow. And I have seen strength come to those who learn from education and the coping experiences of others. At their best, the groups provide community when one's life has been diminished.

In their book, *An Intimate Loneliness*, Gordon Riches and Pam Dawson write about the bereaved, "The benefits of talking—about feelings of grief, about what has happened and what it means—are central to making sense of loss and grief, yet many find it hard to find someone who is prepared to listen." In a bereavement support group, people listen.

A COMPASSIONATE EXPERIENCE

When Karen Snepp traces her grief journey since the death of her brother and only sibling Dave from cancer some twenty years ago, for example, the support she found from The Compassionate Friends sits front and center. Two years older than Karen, Dave was diagnosed with thyroid cancer at age twenty-three. "We were basically told, 'Well, if you're going to get cancer, this is a good one because it's really curable,'" says Karen. "Dave was operated on in the spring of 1978, which was when I graduated from college."

Karen and her brother had attended Purdue at the same time, had even lived in the same dorm for a while. "That said, we were very, very different," she says. "He was cerebral, very contemplative, not an athlete at all, while I . . . " [She laughs] " . . . not that I was stupid, but I wasn't going to compete with him. I was more into sports and ran with my own crowd. Still, Dave and I got along very well. Our family had a cottage in Michigan. One summer, he and I lived there together while working at a tourist place, and we got very close. I mean, I was a sister. I still *am* a sister."

Some years passed and the cancer recurred. This time, it had re-formed around his spine—lower neck, upper back. Radiation held it in check for a while, as did chemotherapy. Karen would make periodic trips from Chicago, where she then lived, to Seattle, where Dave made his home, and the siblings would talk. "In a long-term death, you have a chance to say what needs to be said and do what needs to be done and work through the issues a little bit," says Karen. "What's more, the sibling plays a role in how it's handled. Dave said, 'Don't take me out of the scrapbooks.' He flat out told us that we better remember that he existed." He was thirty-two when he died. And he was not about to be forgotten.

For months afterward, however, Karen found herself unable to share her grief at his passing. "I was not ready to tell anyone that intimate a story because it was so personal an experience and not one that too many people would understand," she says. She did speak to her parents—a difficult task for many surviving siblings, but Karen counts herself fortunate in this regard. "In some ways it helped that I was in Chicago and they were in Philadelphia, so I couldn't see where they were in their grief on a given day," she says. "So if I was speaking with my dad, talking about my inability to concentrate at work, I wasn't there thinking, *Oh, is this a good day for him or a bad day for him?* My parents and I could be very open with one another about how we were feeling about things."

In one of those conversations, Karen's mother mentioned that there was a very active chapter of The Compassionate Friends (TCF), a self-help support organization for family members who've experienced the loss of a child, in Valley Forge, Pennsylvania, not far from where she and her husband lived, and that she wasn't sure if it was a good idea for them to attend a meeting. "It's not like you're signing up for a college course," Karen remembers telling her. "You can go. And if you hate it, you don't need to go back."

She didn't foresee then that TCF would become important not just to her parents but to her own grief journey . . . or that she would someday serve as the organization's national board president—the first sibling to hold that office.

In 1990, two years after Dave's death, Karen had her first exposure to the world of bereavement support when she attended TCF's national conference held that year in Philadelphia. She went mostly to support her parents, but found, she says, "There were sibling workshops along with general workshops that I could attend on topics like anger and grief and long-term illness. There also were sharing sessions. This was the first time I'd had a chance to meet and talk with a significant number of adult siblings who had lost a brother or sister. It was eye-opening.

"There were so many kindred spirits and one in particular, Lisa, whose only brother David had died, and there were two years between them as there'd been between Dave and me. So Lisa and I really connected. The formal sharing session would end at about ten or ten-thirty at night, and then six or seven of us would stay up till two in the morning, in somebody's room, talking. It was very normalizing. I could say to myself: *Okay, I'm not going crazy. It has been two years and it still hurts. There are a lot of other people who feel the way I feel and who can talk about the death of their sister or brother and its impact on the family, its impact on relationships.* It also made me realize how fortunate I was because I didn't have any of the family baggage issues that some siblings were dealing with—such as feeling alone and isolated or unable to talk to their parents." It was her first support group and it was good. In a sense (harking back to the initial advice she gave to her mother to just try a support group), Karen *was* signing up—not just for a course but for what turned out to be the equivalent of a graduate degree.

With another woman, she then started an adult sibling group in Chicago. "It was a core group of about ten people who met once a month, and I facilitated that," Karen says. Periodically, she would also receive calls from the national office in Oak Brook, Illinois, asking if she'd speak with someone who had reached out to TCF for help in coping with the death of a brother or sister. Of course, she agreed. "In moving from the supported to the supporter, I was moving to a different place in my grief," Karen says, describing a pattern evidenced elsewhere in this book, when the one who seeks help becomes strong enough to offer assistance to others. "Interacting with others who had lost a sibling also worked as a kind of gauge of where I was in my own grief. I was able to recognize when the lows were getting less low. My involvement in TCF helped me see what some of those landmarks were.

"The support group provides a benefit of normalizing the grief and helping survivors work through it with people who understand," she says. "At its best, it does even more than that. It becomes like a family."

It has done so for Karen.

NOT FOR EVERYONE

On the other hand, I have spoken with survivors who would not consider joining a group, who feel they could not speak their private pain in a public setting. There also are mourners who benefit best from the special insight to be found in working through their issues in individual therapy—mourners like Jennie. Twenty years ago, when she was twenty-nine, Jennie's younger brother, Lyle, then twenty, died in an accident. "I was broken-hearted," she says. "Friends called, wanting me to go out. I couldn't go out. They just didn't understand and, in many ways, wanted to take me out of myself. But I needed someone to help me explore the grief, to explore all the dynamics of the family. I didn't want Lyle's death to be the kind of traumatic event that would haunt me the rest of my life."

And now?

"I think of my brother every single day," Jennie says, "but sometimes for happy things. He's part of the fabric of my life. It's so hard that this person you shared so much with is gone. Sibling communication is gone. Therapy helped me deal with this."

WHAT A GROUP IS *NOT*

A group provides different support from, and does not take the place of, individual counseling. "Groups are places to work together; they are places where one gives as one takes," says grief counselor Ken Doka. "Not everyone will find a support group suitable; each individual grieves in his or her own way."

Individual therapy and group membership can be helpful complements to each other. Says Sherry Schachter, a grief therapist who has organized and led successful groups for many years: "There are people who do both. Actually it's very good because if something comes up in a support group it can be raised, and really delved into, in therapy."

"Groups are not therapy, but they are therapeutic," says Phyllis Silverman, Ph.D., who specializes in research in bereavement. "I don't like the word 'support' because some people use it literally—to prop you up," she says. "That's not what they are; they are learning centers."

She tells the following story to illustrate the difference: "A woman approached me recently and said, 'I need your opinion.' Her daughter was killed in an accident, and she had been referred to a bereavement group led by a priest in a local church. After the third or fourth week, she found that all he kept doing was telling people, 'Yes, I know this is very hard for you, and that's okay.'

"A good group leader would ask, 'What have you done about that?' And he would ask others in the group how they had dealt with the first birthday following the death, the first Christmas, and so on. *That's* what makes a good support group—it's one where people are going someplace. And it may take some people longer than others, which is okay. But the point is that it's not simply patting them on the back and giving them permission to be miserable."

THE MAKEUP OF AN EFFECTIVE BEREAVEMENT SUPPORT GROUP

Like Phyllis Silverman, Sherry Schachter stresses that it has to be the right support group to be effective. I ask her to share some of the elements that make a group work.

"It helps if it's homogeneous," she says. "I do not like to mix groups. I think surviving spouses should be in one group, parents of lost children should be in another group, adults who've lost their parents should be in a separate group, and people who've lost a sibling should have a group of their own. It's not that one kind of loss is harder or more difficult, it's that they are different and need to be addressed separately. So, for example, there would be different bereavement groups for older spouses and younger spouses. Again, it's not that one is harder or not, but to take someone who was married twelve months and whose husband died and put her in a group with people who've been married fifty years, the issues are very different. She's dealing with the fact that she never had a chance to have children; they're dealing with adult children. They're in different stages of the life cycle."

"What about siblings where your brother died at thirty-two or your brother died at seventy?" I ask.

"I don't separate siblings by age because the relationship is the same," says Schachter. "I do think that people who have lost someone to suicide, however, should be in a separate group because many of the issues are different for those survivors.

"**It should be time-limited** (meaning that the death should be fairly recent). Someone who had a loss ten years ago may still be grieving the death of that person, but they don't belong in a bereavement group. Everyone in my groups has had a recent death—within the past eighteen months. And that's so people can relate to one another. They have still to get over all the firsts without their sibling.

"**It should be educational.** An effective group should be a resource base for gathering information." Those led by Schachter have a psychoeducational component to them. "If we talk about anger one week, the next week I follow up with information on anger and bereavement," she says. Members learn about the grieving process.

"**It should be run by a professional.** There's a lot of controversy about this," Schachter says. "I am not a supporter of groups that are peer-run. I think you need to have someone who has a knowledge base to be able to facilitate a group, to be therapeutic. You can have cofacilitators, so you have one professional, perhaps, and one layperson. But I'm always leery about the credentials of the person running the group because you want to make sure you're in a safe place.

"**You should meet the facilitator.** Going into a group can be difficult. You feel awkward, shy. If you meet someone beforehand, you see a friendly face when you enter the room," she says. "I also think it's important for the clinician to do an intake interview. Some people say they're ready for a group, but when you meet them they can't talk about it. They may need some individual work or maybe they just need some time before joining a group. *There isn't a right time to start.* The intake interview provides the clinician with opportunity to look for complicated grief: Is this person suicidal? Does this person need individual therapy? Does he need a referral in the community? All of these factors are important."

Checking with many existing programs, I find it is not always (or often) possible to meet the facilitator before joining a group. In that case, trust your best instincts (as Karen's mother did), but do go more than once to assess the facilitators and the members and see if the fit works. You may find yourself just listening for a while, and that's okay. An experienced facilitator will know when to respect people's silence, how and when to draw them in.

You will find that groups are either limited to a number of sessions (meeting, for example, once a week for six to ten weeks) or are open-ended. Some have a drop-in format. I prefer groups that are more structured. When members make a commitment to attend, the opportunity exists for continuing friendships to develop. Support groups do not fully resolve grief. That they are effective, however, is seen in the fact that many groups continue informally after their official time has ended.

WHERE TO FIND A GROUP

It may take a little detective work to find an appropriate group. The local hospice or hospital is a good place to start; the bereavement coordinator can offer information and referral to groups in the area.

Funeral homes also sponsor groups, as do many community and religious centers. There are many national groups, like The Compassionate Friends or AARP, as well as cause-specific organizations like Survivors of Suicide, Cancer Care, or Mothers Against Drunk Driving. Some communities have self-help clearinghouses that can provide this information. One can also find support groups online, though these fail to meet several of the criteria given for a successful group. They are helpful, however, in providing survivors with yet another opportunity to tell their story.

Says David Abrams, president and CEO of Hospice Foundation of America, "Finding a group may seem daunting, but it is worth the effort. We have no choice about journeying through grief. We can choose, though, not to journey alone."

Let us go now on that journey with Karen Snepp, who shares her experience and insights on living with loss.

A JOURNEY TO THE "NEW NORMAL"[3]

May 31 marked seven years since my only sibling Dave died from cancer at age thirty-two. This June 28 we would have been celebrating Dave's fortieth birthday with a big party, and I'd be kidding him about going bald, just like all the Snepp men before him. Instead, I'll be getting ready for the TCF National Conference, at which I'll share memories of his brilliance, great smile, and sense of humor with those who will never have the pleasure of meeting him in person.

At this point in my grief journey, most will be good memories of how Dave lived, rather than bad memories of how he died. I can't recall the moment when that shift of perspective occurred, but I would like to share a few memories and milestones that have marked the way:

- Months after Dave died, I went to the movie "Big," starring Tom Hanks and "lost it" when his mother stared out the window wondering if she'd ever see him again. I watched the movie recently and didn't lose it.
- It was three months before I felt up to sharing with anyone the details of the day my brother died at his home in Bellevue, Washington, in the company of Mom, Dad, and me. On the way home from that emotional conversation, I drove the wrong way down a one-way street in downtown Chicago—it might be smart to have a friend drive you to your first few TCF meetings!
- I discovered that the grief path is not a straight line. A few good days can be followed by several bad ones. I've heard other TCF members call this their "roller coaster ride."
- For a year, I couldn't keep the radio on if "Wind Beneath My Wings" came on. For the next year, I kept it on but cried through it. Now, I can usually make it all the way through without any tears!
- With the help of TCF, I realized that despite friends expecting it to be possible, I'd never be "back to normal." My focus instead shifted to finding my "new normal." While I can't point to a time when that happened (probably after the 1990 TCF conference), THAT was a milestone.
- For three Christmases after Dave died, I didn't put up a tree in my condo. For Christmas 1991, as I was getting out ornaments for my first tree since

[3]Reprinted by permission of the author, Karen Snepp, and *We Need Not Walk Alone*, the national magazine of The Compassionate Friends. © 1995.

his death, I came across a bunch of ornaments that he had had in his apartment. I came totally unglued then, but now I look forward to seeing those ornaments each Christmas.

- It was three years before I felt that I had enough emotional energy to pursue a relationship. Even now, I don't have a lot of tolerance for guys I go out with that gripe about their brothers or sisters.

My most vivid "landmark" to date along my grief journey came in February 1993. Following my Dad's father's death in December 1992, we were in Atlanta cleaning out my grandfather's apartment, and I came across a pile of postcards and letters that Dave had written to my grandparents through the years. Earlier in my journey, a "blind side" such as that would have sent me into a tailspin. In this case, though, my immediate reaction was one of happiness, for I had found a part of Dave that I didn't know I still had! I saved a few of the postcards, sent a couple to my cousin who was referenced in some of the letters, and (amazingly) threw the rest away. It was fun to share the memories, but I didn't feel the need to hang on to them. It was at that point, nearly five years after Dave's death, that I truly felt as if I was closing in on that "new normal."

CHAPTER 9

Resolving a Discordant Relationship

"When a loved one dies" . . . "dealing with the loss of a loved one" . . . These are the phrases most commonly used when speaking about the death of someone with close ties to the survivor. The connection is acknowledged and love is presumed.

In reality, most relationships are more complicated than that, especially when it comes to our siblings. As kids, we are thrown together. Later in life, some of us are not able to grow beyond childhood rivalry and resentments and carry the conflict of early years into adulthood. Others develop a distant cordiality with a sister or brother, meeting mostly at family weddings and funerals—in some cases, not even then. We tell ourselves, "It's better that way." Sometimes, our brother or sister acts in a manner that leads us to opt out of the relationship, to sever the ties, or they're the ones who choose to break the connection over slights real or imagined. One might think, then, that the death of a sister or brother with whom one is less than fully loving or from whom one is estranged would have few consequences. The reality is much more complicated, as is the grief process for these mourners.

Barry describes having "a bipolar relationship" with his late brother, Jeff, explaining, "When it was good, it was very good, but when it was bad it was horrid." Jeff was thirty-five when he was killed in an auto accident. Barry was then forty. "Jeff was a dysfunctional guy," says Barry. "In a way, his death made things easier for me. Still . . . " His voice trails off.

"I did not love my brother, I did not like my brother, I was only so sorry to hear that he had died, I was comforted to hear other people say that they were sorry he had died," writes Jamaica Kincaid in a memoir about her younger brother, Devon, who died at thirty-three of AIDS. She did not like her brother, yet it helped her to hear expressions of condolence. Why? "Someone I did not know I loved had died."

"Your siblings are part of your identity," says grief specialist P. Gill White. "So it doesn't matter if you get along with them or not. When they die, it feels like something left you. Physically left you. It can be very painful."

Years ago we used to think that people who had ambivalent or angry relationships did not have to grieve. In fact, studies show they often go through complicated grieving in which they regret not only the death of their distant sibling but rue the fact that there is no longer any possibility for reconciliation—no chance to rework the relationship, to forgive or be forgiven.

In a moving memoir, *Landscape without Gravity*, Barbara Lazear Ascher speaks to this point concerning the death of her younger brother, Bobby, of AIDS, at age thirty-one. Her grief is all the more difficult, she finds, because she and her brother were at odds in the last years preceding his death. A friend accuses her of carrying sadness too far. "You can't possibly be grieving," she says. "You and your brother weren't even that close."

Ascher writes: "My friend was not wrong; my brother and I were not close. The passion of our attachment when he was a young boy turned to later disenchantment. Now that old passion returns and fuels my remorse. I turn the anger, the integral aspect of grief, against myself.... Why hadn't I been larger-hearted? ... Why had there been limits and conditions on my love? ... Now I am ashamed of myself. Such guilt and ambivalence complicate and extend grief. But how could an outsider understand that no, my brother and I were not close, and that is precisely why I grieve."

For the author, writing about her brother and their difficult relationship was cathartic.

STILL WORKING IT OUT

Three years have passed since my friend Hedda, sixty-two, lost her younger brother and only sibling, Stuart, to pancreatic cancer. I ask her if she'll talk to me about it, and she readily says yes, then twice changes the date and time appointed for our interview. When we do speak, she seems flustered. Normally poised and highly articulate, she starts out telling me about their childhood, describing it as very close. "We were always running around screaming, getting into trouble, getting into fights in the back of the car, that sort of thing," she says. "We were constant companions. I was my father's favorite, he was my mother's."

Their lives diverged as they got older. "I was the stalwart person and he was the screwup," she says. "He was part of the whole sixties scene, and I was straitlaced." They grew up and each married. "He disdained money and I was a rich person. He questioned my values and made me feel shitty. With all that, he was the only person I could talk to when I had problems in my marriage or with my kids. And yet... and yet... I am so *angry* with him. When our parents became older and ill, he did practically nothing. Never, never did he offer to help. Then he got cancer and died within two years of being diagnosed." She speaks of his death as "the worst thing that ever happened to me." In the next breath, she says, "He was both my support and my critic. It's complicated.

"I once read that somebody who was widowed would dress in her husband's clothes," she says. "So what I do is... I have this shirt of his, it's an old shirt that my sister-in-law gave me. Around the time of his birthday (I feel crummy around his birthday), I sleep in it. It reminds me of him and it's good."

"It sounds as if you're still having a hard time with this," I say.

"Yes, it's still ongoing," she says, and begins to cry. "It's ongoing in a way that I don't understand. But how can you resolve a relationship when the other party's not around?"

Later, I ask the question of grief counselor Ken Doka: How *do* you resolve a discordant or ambivalent relationship with a brother or sister once that sibling has died?

"It's hard to give a blanket prescription to people," he says. "If I were a grief counselor with a person, I would explore the relationship that they had with the individual who died. I would explore the roots of it. Once you acknowledge that there is some unfinished business, there may be opportunities to find ways to finish it: it may be some kind of ritual of reconciliation, it could be anything from speaking to an empty chair to writing a letter to participating in some kind of therapeutic ritual.

Those sorts of things have to be individually designed and tailored. But they can be done."

THE SEARCH FOR MEANING

I next speak with Marian Sandmaier, whose grief at her brother Bob's death, at age thirty-three, led her to embark on an exploration of the positive and negative influences that siblings have on our lives, which she discusses in her book, *Original Kin: The Search for Connection among Adult Sisters and Brothers.*

Marian was the second of four children; her brother Bob was the third. "Growing up, Bob was my archenemy," she says. "He was four years younger, but from an early age he was so aggressive and so smart—he had a way of conniving and tricking and getting on top, which he used against all family members. Obviously, he was very troubled, but we siblings were too young to understand that he was anything but an impediment in our lives. Because I was the only one who would oppose him, we were head-to-head a whole lot."

The friction continued into adulthood, when any chance for growing closeness was complicated by geographic distance (Marian lived in Philadelphia, Bob in San Francisco) and lifestyle choices. In her book, she describes seeing her brother's life "explode like fireworks, over and over and over again, as he gambled untold thousands of dollars, totaled his cars, confronted guns in his face, dove into alcohol and cocaine, walked into and away from recovery programs . . . "

"He developed a back problem at work one day and a friend lent him a half-filled bottle of codeine in liquid form," Marian tells me. "Only months before he had entered a treatment program to defeat the dual addictions to cocaine and alcohol and had emerged with a written recovery plan that plainly stated: *No mind-altering substances.* Four days later, he was found dead on his living room couch. He had ingested all of the codeine. I don't think that he did it on purpose. I had spoken to him on the phone five days before, and he was very upbeat. His friends corroborated this.

"I wouldn't describe our relationship as discordant when he died," she says. "It certainly was earlier, but by the time he died I would have described it as too distant for my liking. Bobbie was the kind of person I had to defend myself against all my life, so I could never admit to myself that I cared about him that much. He was certainly not the center of my life or my need for close relationships. I wasn't invested in him in that way. We never had time in our lives to be close and comfortable. *And that's what I was mourning at the end.*"

"The task is a complicated one," write Stephen Bank and Michael Kahn in the introduction to the fifteenth anniversary edition of their book, *The Sibling Bond.* "If one's sibling has died and the relationship was unresolved, it is even more wrenching emotionally, for the time has run out before one thought it would."

Unexpected grieving: "My response to Bob's death was terrible," Marian continues, "and that surprised nobody more than me. I had physical symptoms, and I developed"—she laughs—"a terrible back problem, to the point where I was twisted up physically. I didn't connect that to my brother's death because I still thought I didn't care. At some point I visited a massage therapist. She saw me all twisted up in this knot and she said something like, 'If you could cry about something, what would it be?' And I burst into tears. I knew I was crying about my brother. This sounds like hocus-pocus, but that twisted back resolved within forty-eight hours.

"But then there was this new process, one that evolved over several years, of re-evaluating the relationship with my brother. I began to realize that in spite of our mutual aggression and opposition, he and I were actually alike. We were the only ones who rebelled against stuff that was going on in our family that we didn't like. So the regret was that: one, Bob died; two, there was no time to build the relationship with him that I wanted and thought I needed; and three, that I didn't *know* I needed until after he died. That's how I learned I needed him. *That was the grief.* I may have been depressed about that for close to three years."

Seeking and finding better memories was helpful: At some point, Marian's husband, Dan, said to her, "You know, Bob would have wanted to be close to you. This isn't just a one-sided yearning. You already had a relationship and he knew it." Says Marian, "Dan made me feel that Bob and I really weren't in life as distant and unable to touch each other as I thought. And Dan told me some stories that reminded me of times when Bob and I did connect. Remembering those moments of closeness was very, very important. That was also a big turning point."

She waits a while, then says, "You know, there's also something here about the preciousness of one's own life. When a sibling dies, it's a peer and it comes much closer to the bone. A thirty-three-year-old,

6′4″, strapping 200-pounder could be gone one day. It could happen. Bob's death not only gave me a message to make the most of my own life, but it made me more aware of the importance in my life of my remaining siblings. I'm much closer to my sister Donna and I would say that my brother Phil and I definitely have made progress. We're tiptoeing around it, but I'm conscious that it's important."

CHAPTER 10

The Legacy of Loss in Childhood

"My brother's death has shadowed my entire life."

—Sanford J. Ungar

Among the many survivors with whom I speak are several who tell of having been very young when their brother or sister died. For some among them, actual memories of the deceased are sketchy, for others they are finely etched. Even if the time shared with the sibling was brief, however, they find that losing a sibling in childhood leads to consequences that are lifelong.

THE REPLACEMENT CHILD

Such is the case with Sanford Ungar, although he never got to spend any time at all with his brother, Calvin, whose death took place *before* Sanford was born. In 1944, Calvin Ungar, a twenty-year-old navigator in the Army Air Forces, died in a military plane crash over Italy. His parents, who also had three daughters, were bereft about losing their cherished only son and determined to fill the unbearable void in their life. Within the year, they had another son. "I am that replacement child," says Ungar, sixty-three, now president of Goucher College in Baltimore, Maryland.

"I grew up in the shadow of a brother I could never meet or know," he says. "I don't know that I would call it a hardship; it was just a circumstance... although his name came up every day when I was a young child. I aimed to be the most loving of children, hoping this might buy me a reprieve from hearing about him."

Growing up in the shadow meant dealing with a father who "was very bruised by the experience of losing a son" and a mother who continued to mourn. "I used to hate February because of what was coming," Ungar recalls. "My brother's birthday fell on February 28th, and my mother would dress in black for weeks in advance. I wished I could change his birthday to February 29th, so then it would be observed only every four years."

Growing up in the shadow also meant competing with a perfect ghost. As has been earlier mentioned, most of us experience some sense of rivalry with our siblings. We look to identify ways in which we excel "as compared to . . . " For Ungar, Calvin's reputation was unassailable. By repute, he'd been a top student, a debater, a popular fellow. "I felt obliged to compete with Calvin in school and everywhere else," Ungar says. "It's not that I worried in any way about being undervalued; it's just that he set this unmatchable standard because it couldn't be tested. You couldn't check him out to see if there were any flaws."

His sister Mimi, twelve years his senior, was extremely helpful. "I was sort of her mascot," says Ungar. "She's the one, certainly the earliest one, to help me understand that I didn't have to live in my brother's shadow and could be a person in my own right." That realization has been reinforced by age and achievement, permitting the replacement child to develop an appreciation of his brother as an actual person instead of a sacred legend.

CHILDHOOD LOSS/LIFETIME MOURNING

This kind of deification of the deceased occurs frequently when children die young, creating a burden for the surviving child: How could one hope to measure up? As Brenda remembers it, "My sister was a paragon. Dead, she had no flaws." Brenda was six when it was discovered that her older sister, Louise, eight, had a brain tumor. Understandably, her parents were caught up in caring for the critically ill child . . . and for their infant son who'd been born a month earlier. But Brenda was not at an age for understanding. "I remember riding around and around in circles on my bicycle . . . nobody paying attention to me," Brenda says. After Louise died, Brenda's father sought relief in work. Through the thin wall that separated her bedroom from her parents' room, the young girl would hear her mother sobbing night after night. It reinforced the six-year-old's belief (common to many surviving siblings, also noted in Chapter 3) that the wrong child had died.

"My sister was the wanted first child," she says. "For their second child my parents hoped for a son, so I was not favored in the first place. Of course I felt that the wrong child had died. Also, I now became the oldest, with all of the responsibility but none of the honor of having been born into that role."

Decades passed before Brenda dealt with this issue in therapy, which proved very helpful. "I was surprised that it came up and that there was still so much pain," she says.

The ache doesn't go away. That is the message conveyed by Amanda, a thirty-two-year-old woman who contacted me when she heard of this project and who has been struggling with the memory of her brother's life and death, at the age of ten, for more than eighteen years. It was one of those tragedies that make the headlines: Amanda, then fourteen, and Floyd had gone on a day trip to New York's Jones Beach with an older cousin and her boyfriend, and Floyd drowned. Amanda remembers trying to alert the lifeguards to the fact that her brother was in the water . . . remembers that they didn't take her seriously until it was too late. "Right after he died, I blocked out a lot of what happened that day," she says. "But I was left with extreme guilt. I don't know if I'll ever be able to shake this in a lifetime."

What helped was a stranger on the beach, a woman who had seen what had occurred and who quickly came over and put her arms around the shaken youngster. "She was my guardian angel," Amanda says. "She kept in touch with me and saw me many times thereafter. It turned out that she'd had a brother die in a motorcycle accident and so she understood that I needed someone to be with me." Amanda's parents were less supportive. For a long time, they would not talk about Floyd, the youngest of their four children. No photographs of him were displayed in their home.

DELAYED MOURNING

When Amanda was sixteen, she started going to a counselor—against her parents' wishes. (They may have believed that seeing a mental health professional was a sign of weakness, she thinks.) And she went on with her life. Then, when she turned thirty, she had a breakdown. Suddenly, she found herself mourning all over again. She's not sure what triggered it. "It may be that I had hit a milestone birthday and was thinking about having a family of my own someday. It may be that the family dog, bought soon after my brother died, passed away, and some of the unresolved feelings from my childhood came back. If I do go on to marry and have children, I'll probably find myself mourning again when that child turns ten. It's an ongoing fact of my life. I'm currently creating a Web site to honor my brother's memory, and I hope that will help me to deal with my grief, but I'm still unable to talk about him with others."

The delayed mourning that Amanda experienced at the age of thirty, when she had her breakdown, is not an unusual occurrence for survivors who were relatively young when their siblings died. As P. Gill White explains, "If you're a child when you lose a sibling, you are to a degree protected by your magical thinking." Later in life, the reality of that loss may be recalled more strongly, with the result that grief hits you when you least expect it and when others in your life are unlikely to understand what you're going through or to offer solace.

White speaks from experience. She was fifteen and her sister Linda was thirteen when the younger girl complained of a pain in her side and was found to have rhabdomyosarcoma, a rare kind of cancer that usually hits much younger children. In the four months between diagnosis and death, Pleasant helped care for her sister both at home and in the hospital. "We were so close, and everyone could see that we couldn't function without one another," she told me. Still, she says, "I was glad that she had died because she was in such agony. It's like watching somebody being tortured. You don't want it to go on."

As for Pleasant, "I went on," she says, "and was pretty much fine—I didn't think about it much or anything—until my own children got to be about that age. When my son reached the age of thirteen and my daughter was ten . . . and they were having a fight one day, and one of them called the other a name . . . it all came rushing back to me: my childhood and the loss of my sister. There was such a big gap from when my sister died and when I addressed it. But it actually happens. You repress it until you're strong enough to deal with it, and then it comes back. *That's* when I started trying to find a therapist."

It was not an easy task. "One therapist actually said to me, 'You should be over that by now.' And another one said, 'Oh, there must be something else. You can't feel that bad from losing a sibling.' I was so angry that I was motivated to become a therapist myself."

A secret grief: In her book, *Unspoken Grief: Coping with Childhood Sibling Loss*, psychotherapist Helen Rosen observes that the death of a sibling in childhood is not something that adult survivors generally discuss. "In fact," she writes, "it is highly likely that a number of individuals known to the reader have experienced such a loss without having shared that information."

I find that Rosen is right. When I mentioned to friends that I was working on this book, a number of them offered, "Why not interview me?" I'd known them for years, had attended their celebrations, and thought I knew their families. But I had not known—because they'd never mentioned it—that their family had included another member, that there was a brother or sister who died in childhood.

So it was with my friend Simone (an only child, I thought) who, upon hearing of my interest in sibling loss, volunteered that once upon a time she'd had an older sister. We talk.

"My sister's death affected my whole life and does so still," says Simone, with great gravity. A handsome woman who not long ago celebrated her eightieth birthday, when we speak she is back in Vienna and the time is 1930.

"My sister Lili was nine and a half and I was five when she died of complications of appendicitis," Simone says. "She was sick one day, she went to the hospital the second day, and she died the third day. It was the first trauma of my life—without any doubt, even though I have no conscious memory of my sister. What I do remember is my mother and my aunt returning from the cemetery (I did not go to the funeral).... And they told me that I would never see my sister again. They did not explain anything; who talked to a five-year-old in those days? From then on the subject of my sister was a closed topic." Unfortunately, this is an all-too-common response on the part of parents. A sibling dies in childhood—and the surviving children understand that the subject is taboo.

"This much I know," says Simone. "My parents changed, my life changed."

She goes on: "Lili was known in my family as the paragon of virtue. She was the good one and I was the bad one—a reputation that stuck to me. When I asked my mother many years later *why* that reputation... what did I do that was so bad... my mother could only remember one thing. In Austria there are separate greetings that you say as a child to a grown-up and to a servant. One is more polite—*I kiss your hand Madame*, which is what children say to grown-ups. To friends and servants or the mailman or the concierge, you have a different greeting. This is what my mother came up with—that I used the 'servant' greeting to all the ladies who were her friends. *That* was my bad behavior."

Like Brenda, Simone suffered from survivor's guilt. "I did feel that the wrong child had died because Lili was the good one. I couldn't compete with her. I was very close to my mother, but I always felt that I did not fulfill her expectations, no matter what I did. So I probably did all sorts of things I shouldn't have done, because that is what was expected of me."

Simone survived the war years as a hidden child. "I'm very lucky," she says. "I know that, but I never felt very lucky. I felt, and still feel, like an outsider, like that lost little sibling."

"What helped you?" I ask Simone, for I know her to be an accomplished and independent woman.

"My late husband," she answers. "He sent me into therapy. He changed my life. But most of all he accepted me as I am."

She has spent a lifetime seeking the acceptance that eluded her as a child.

ONE DEATH, TWO RESPONSES

Though there are commonalities in the grief experience for children, there's no question that there also are differences, depending on such variables as age when the sibling died, their understanding of the event, closeness to the deceased (including whether they shared a room), parental response, availability of people and programs to help one deal with grief. To gain some insight into how differently the same death might be experienced, I speak with sisters Maggie Meigs, fifty-three, second child and oldest daughter of eight Gerner siblings, and Jackie Jones, forty, the family's youngest, about the death of their brother, Arthur, when he was six.

Maggie, fifteen when it happened, shares her recollection of how Arthur died: "It was Friday afternoon of the Memorial Day weekend. For Minneapolis, where the family was then living, it was a fairly warm day. My parents were sitting out back of our home and talking, maybe having a drink. The next thing I knew, our neighbor Joe came running up the alleyway, shouting for my parents to come quickly—Arthur had been in an accident. (What happened was that he'd been riding my brother David's bicycle, had come to the end of the alley, and was hit by a car driven by a secretary at my school.) I ran up the alley with my parents.

All these years I have never recovered the memory of seeing Arthur, although I know that I did. It was so traumatic.

"I remember seeing my baby sister Jackie, who was then three, and I remember thinking *I'll take her home*, which I did. When our parents returned from the hospital, they told us that Arthur was dead."

Jackie remembers: hearing the neighbor's shout, then running up the alley behind her parents. "Arthur was on the ground," she recalls. "My mom was bent over him. She was doing CPR. I remember someone saying, 'Get the kids back.' I guess at this point I got taken away. I can tell you that everything, from the second I saw Arthur to the second I forget, is black and white at this point. I remember color when I was in the back yard . . . but the incident itself was black and white for me. Still to this day that's how I remember it. I remember no blood. There was blood, but I didn't see it. I don't remember anything else until I was five. Arthur was my buddy. I did everything with him. I took baths with him. He was my total playmate. I'm told I acted out, but I don't remember it. I didn't know what death meant." It wasn't in her vocabulary yet.

Maggie remembers: "They took my brother to the hospital, and then at the funeral there was a closed casket, so we never saw him again. I vividly recall thinking, *What am I supposed to do? Should I cry or not cry?* I really didn't know how to act."

What Maggie remembers most of all was the change in her family. "We went in an instant from being this normal, average, happy, big old family to total chaos, total brokenness. My dad coped by working harder. Both parents took to drinking in order to help them get through things. Their marriage suffered. We kids were pretty much left to our own devices."

Jackie remembers: "My sister Dorothy was my caretaker. She's six years older, and I have the feeling that she was attached to me even before I was born. After Arthur was killed, I think Dorothy's instinct to take care of me got stronger as my mom grew weaker."

Maggie, too, took on a caretaker role, one she now regards as inappropriate for a surviving child. "The biggest mistake I made in my life was trying to 'fix' my parents' pain," she says. "I acted in ways that I hoped would change them back to happy, whole people again. I know now that it was not my responsibility to do this. By trying to make them better, I stuffed a lot of my own sadness, fears, and worries inside and developed a kind of sardonic humor to cover up the pain I was feeling. It was years before I was able to let the tears flow. Then I cried for

Arthur because he was dead and I missed him; I cried for myself because of all *I* had missed. I missed the attention my parents were no longer able to give me as they went their separate ways. I missed the years of carefree childhood that had been ripped away. I missed feeling safe and secure."

What helped: "I had to figure out that it was essential to deal with my own feelings," she goes on. "The origins of my becoming a psychologist are in this pain. So at the age of twenty-four I went for counseling. It was absolutely helpful. Seeing my mom take control of herself, give up the drinking, and get involved in Compassionate Friends and Bereaved Parents also helped. All of a sudden we could talk about Arthur. We could acknowledge birthdays and anniversaries and tell funny stories. You will never find people with as big and compassionate hearts as my siblings."

Jackie is still struggling. When she was fourteen years old, Jackie experienced a second significant loss when Dorothy's daughter, Emily, a cherished niece, died of liver disease at age three. "I was there for Emily from the moment she was born," says Jackie. "I would wheel her in her carriage. I took her horseback riding. I did everything with her. She was born perfect, then she got sick and, six weeks later, she died." The teenaged Jackie was devastated.

The adult she became is wary. "I can't tell you that I ever learned how to cope," she says. "With Arthur's death, my parents' divorce, my niece's death . . . I have learned that people might die and I might hurt. My job as a paramedic reinforces that. As a result, I get close to people to a certain extent and then I put up a brick wall. That makes it very hard to be married and very hard to be a parent," she says, although she is both. (Daughter Emily, who is named for her niece, is six years old.) "It's something I still have to work on."

HELP FOR SURVIVING CHILDREN

In *The Sibling Bond*, Bank and Kahn conclude that children who lose their siblings during the childhood years should be worked with individually, with their parents, and in support groups of brothers and sisters. They write, "Leadership must come from the medical and psychological community in organizing such opportunities if we are to enable families to free themselves, their children, and future generations of the silent but destructive ghost of a person who has died too young."

I learn about Heartlight, a bereavement program at Children's Memorial Hospital in Chicago that addresses this issue by offering much-needed support and a safe place for families to be together while coping with the death of a child. As we know, family members tend to grieve in their own way and in their own time. The importance of programs designed especially for children is that they pay attention to the young mourners at a time when the significant adults in their life are likely to be most distracted.

I speak with Kristin James, a licensed clinical professional counselor and coordinator of the Heartlight program.

"If the loss of a sibling occurred when you were a child, then how your family grieved, how your family supported each other and coped with that loss is going to directly affect how you integrate that into your identity, into your relationships as you grow to adulthood," she says. (Certainly the stories recounted here support that finding.)

I ask her to provide some examples of how families grieve, along with the likely consequences for surviving siblings.

She replies: "Take a family who had very open communication, who were very honest with their children at the time of death, about what caused the death, what's going to happen next, a family that allowed the children to grieve openly, whether it's through crying, questions, a family that could tolerate the grief of their children. . . . To the degree that a family supports the siblings when they're young at the time of loss, it allows those children to have positive relationships, positive self-esteem as they grow up and beyond.

"Contrast that with a family where the parents may have been so overwhelmed in their own grief, where they couldn't tolerate the physical and emotional responsibilities of raising the surviving siblings," she continues. "Then you may have a child who quickly takes on the responsibility of nurturing the other siblings. Well, that's directly going to affect them into adulthood. . . . Or a child who is never allowed to grieve or to ask questions about why somebody died. That's going to bring into adulthood a more general sense of mistrust of others because those questions, those feelings were never resolved at the time of loss. There are many adults, for example, who were not told as children why somebody died, but have continued to grow up with a vague understanding of *My sister was sick, but I don't know what she was sick from.* Often they become hypochondriacs because all they know is that somebody got sick and then they died."

I raise the issue of children who were told "Your brother passed" or "He's now in heaven" instead of "He died."

"Yes, there needs to be honesty," says James. "But you also have to explain the word *died.* Some children don't understand what that means. And why it happened. They may wonder: Was it something that *I* can get? Was it something that *I* did wrong? Children are by nature egocentric. So if someone doesn't take the opportunity to tell them what happened, they may continue for years feeling on some level that the death was their fault."

A CHILD-CENTERED STRATEGY HELPS

This could very well have happened in the Teibel family, whom we meet next, following the loss of the youngest child, Drew, to SIDS (Sudden Infant Death Syndrome) when he was eight and a half months old. His big brother Max, then not quite eight, went in one morning to wake the baby and found him unmoving. A middle brother, Philip, had yet to celebrate his fifth birthday. The kinds of rituals that parents Pamela and Howard Teibel have established, the safeguards they have instituted to help their sons deal with the tragedy, may be instructive for others.

Untimely death had visited Pamela before. At the age of eighteen, she was wakened one night to be told that her brother, Ned, twenty-three, had been killed in a car accident. Her grief lasted for years, then subsided, only to return intensified when her baby died. "It was very much like my brother's automobile accident—just out of nowhere," she says, "and I went off the deep end. I walked through the funeral like a robot, then went home to bed and stayed there for weeks." Support and grief counseling not only helped Pamela get through but enabled her to address the needs of her surviving sons.

"After my brother died, the thing that was incredibly difficult for me was that within twenty-four hours a priest had come to the house and he put his hand on my shoulder and said, 'Be strong for your parents,' and I thought that meant, as a good kid, to just not show any emotion. So after my son died, I was very clear that my kids would be allowed to feel what they felt.

"Kids like rituals, so we established some very specific traditions with our boys around birthdays and holidays. The first year on the anniversary of Drew's death, we took them to a hotel because we didn't want them to wake up replaying the memory of that morning. I wanted new memories in place of the memories of that day. From that first year forward, however, we decided to hold a party at the house for all of our neighbors and good friends and do a balloon release. It gives everybody the opportunity to remember Drew in a joyous way. It's been good for our children and for their friends. On Drew's birthday we go out to dinner because that's what we do on birthdays. Max and Philip each get to invite a friend or two, and after dinner we head to Barnes & Noble where they pick out books, which we donate to the school library in Drew's memory.

"Both boys have been in therapy, and they know they can go back if ever they feel the need," says Pamela. "The other thing I've done is that I stay in touch with my sons' guidance counselors and their teachers, particularly around the anniversary date each year. I ask the teachers to please keep an eye on them and if they notice any difficulty to let me know. Some people may think I'm crazy, but knowing what I went through . . . [She laughs] . . . *I* don't think I'm crazy."

BENEFITS OF SUPPORT GROUPS FOR CHILDREN

Where Pamela's sons have benefited from individual therapy, children may also be helped by membership in a bereavement support group. At Heartlight, as at other successful bereavement programs, parents meet in one group while siblings meet separately, divided developmentally, from age four through high school.

The group helps youngsters in several ways, as Kristin James explains: "Meeting with other children who had a similar experience with death both normalizes and validates it. There are very few other places in your life—whether you're a child or a grown-up—that somebody can understand that loss.

"It's separate from their parents, it's confidential and it's safe, so they can ask those questions or exhibit emotions that would not be tolerated at home. There are some children who may not be able to say their sister or brother's name at home or talk about the funeral. Or say that they're *relieved* that a brother or sister died because now Mom isn't gone every day. That can be very difficult for a parent to help a child acknowledge, whereas peers can make that possible.

"It provides children with other ways of expressing their feelings or coping with them—through music, writing, art. Within the group, they are given an opportunity to use a variety of tools."

DEALING WITH *YOUR* UNRESOLVED GRIEF

As we have seen, children who experience a sibling's death and do *not* benefit from such early and informed intervention by parents or helping professionals often become adults who must then deal with their unresolved grief.

What *can* help: There are opportunities in adulthood to go back, says James, and people who struggle with unanswered questions should seize them. "You can, for example, go back to your parents and say, 'I was sent away the week after my sister died. What really happened?'"

I think: Simone would have liked to know about her sister's funeral, but she has *filled in some of the blanks. She's gone back to Europe and located her sister's grave. It was overgrown by grass, but she cleared the ground somewhat and now has a photograph of it among her keepsakes.*

"Sometimes it's even just gathering memories, whether it's from a parent or a family friend or relative. Maybe you've lost a lot of your memories of the sibling who died . . . ," says James.

I think of Sanford Ungar, the replacement child, who in the past few years has heard from and welcomed contact with people who knew his brother and were willing to share their memories of the real Calvin, someone with strengths and weaknesses.

"In adulthood, there are still opportunities to go back and gather memories, gather stories, get your questions answered," James says. "That's a significant part of the healing process regardless of how old you are and how long ago the loss was."

CHAPTER 11

When the Spirit Moves You

I am an active dreamer. I dream often, in color, and in great detail. Every once in a while, I dream about my sister. When I wake up, I turn to my husband and say, smiling, "I just had a visit from Sybil."

"Isn't that nice," he replies.

And it is.

Other mourners mention to me that they, too, have vivid dreams about their late siblings. They go on to describe their dreams as helping them maintain a connection to the sister or brother who has died.

Sylvie, fifty-two, married, with two college-age youngsters, shares her story and her dreams:

"Twelve years ago, I lost my youngest brother, Greg, just fifteen days before his twenty-seventh birthday. He was ten years younger than I and our relationship was more like mother/son than brother/sister, although we had that relationship as well. He was found dead on the floor of his living room. Greg had been diagnosed with epilepsy when he was two, but it was controlled by medication. He'd had no grand mal seizures. And he led an active life. Five years later, I read an article about Sudden Unexplained Death from Epilepsy, and I think that's what must have happened to Greg. His death was shocking and devastating.

"I have dreams. In one dream I found myself in this quarry. He was there, and I said, 'Oh my God, Greg, you're here!' And he said, 'Yeah. And I have something really important to teach you. I want you to fly.' And I said, 'Fly?' I mean, I've always wanted to fly. And so he taught me. The quarry dropped off, and I was free and flying and having an awesome time. Then I woke up and I was elated because it seemed so real to me.

"I can remember a dream where I was driving in a car and I looked next to me, and Greg appeared. And we just had a conversation. . . . On my birthday he's appeared in my dreams twice to wish me a happy birthday. . . . And once, in a waking state, I was thinking about a dream—I must have had one—and I remember thinking, *I never tell him how much I love him.* So in the next dream where I saw him, I walked into a house—it was totally unfamiliar to me; it was a small, humble house—and there was a kitchen table with a red checkered cloth on it. Greg was sitting on a chair behind the table, and I said, 'Greg, I love you.' I kept saying it, over and over. He smiled and said, 'I know.' And that was the end of the dream. When I woke up, I thought, *I remembered to say I love you.*"

"They are dreams that comforted me," she says.

When I listen to grief professionals or look at the literature on bereavement, what stands out for me is the emphasis on the salutary effect of continuing bonds with the deceased, the understanding that it is important to keep the people we love alive in memory, whether through relic or ritual. I am surprised, however, when a fair number of surviving siblings describe phenomenal happenings or when they tell me about having received after-death communications from the one who has died. The belief that the dead live on in some form or spirit is very comforting for the mourners.

AFTER-DEATH COMMUNICATIONS

"I know this sounds bizarre," says Sylvie, "but I don't feel like my brother is gone. Greg still exists; it's just not in the world that *I* live in. I don't believe in heaven in the biblical sense, but I do believe in an existence in another form."

Sylvie then shares another visit from her brother, this one occurring when she was awake. "Following Greg's death, I had to fly from Boston to Illinois to join my mother and father. At that point, I was almost crippled by flying in airplanes. I'm on the plane, tears in my eyes, and I look out the window and there's a rainbow. Now we were thirty-five thousand feet up—too high for rainbows. I asked the passenger seated next to me, 'Do you see that?' And he said, 'What?' It was such a clear rainbow, but he didn't see it. So I felt that it was Greg watching over me. This rainbow followed me all the way to St. Louis.

For the return flight, I took a small, eight-seater plane to Peoria, and the rainbow was back. . . . There have been odd times when we see rainbows that coincide with things going on in our lives. I firmly believe it's Greg. So there definitely were signs. They stopped after about eight years. I almost feel that he knows that I don't need him to take care of me anymore, that I've come to terms with his passage from this world."

Louis LaGrand, Ph.D., a noted grief counselor, has written widely on the subject of after-death communications, which, he explains, are common, unexplainable scientifically, come in various guises, and result in meaningful assistance to the beneficiary. He writes, "Consolation in time of sadness and remorse appears to be the most logical reason for the ADC experience."

Certainly that applies to the incident related by Russell Stiller (see Chapter 6), who interrupted writing the eulogy for his brother Stephen and stepped outside into a moonless night when, out of nowhere, a beach ball came toward him. The only explanation Russell could find for a ball to be shooting out of a parking lot at that moment was "it had to be Stephen."

Anita Korsonsky, another 9/11 survivor, is convinced that her sister Jeanette lives on. "I think she is reaching out to me—I know this sounds weird—in little different ways," she says. "Say I'm in a store and I'm looking for a card for my friend's birthday and my eyes immediately light on Happy Birthday Sister cards. I know this is my sister and she's thinking about me and this is her little sign. Or I'm in a store that sells picture frames, and I see one that says Sister. Maybe I'm subconsciously looking for it, but to me it's her sign saying that she's thinking of me. Things like that used to freak me out a little, but now I just think, *Hi Jeanette. You must be here with me.* It's weird, but it's a beautiful thing."

Anita's response touches me because since my sister died I have been unable to go near the Sister section in a greeting card store, to find the kind of comfort in connection that Heather Summerhayes Cariou, whose sister Pam fought a valiant struggle against cystic fibrosis, describes to me.

"When Pam died, it was just so inexplicable to me that she could stop," says Heather. "The body stops but that energy has to go somewhere. I feel her around me quite often, though not as often as I used to. For a while after she died, I didn't feel her around me, though I longed for her. It's almost the more I've allowed myself to be released from the grip of the desire to be with her again that she has re-entered.

"I'll tell you two stories.

"One: Writing the book about our relationship [*Sixtyfive Roses*] was very long and painful and joyful and everything else. When I finished the first draft and put The End on it, I realized that it was March 28, Pam's birthday. Pure coincidence. I took the manuscript, went over to Kinko's (this was in Los Angeles) and I had the manuscript replicated. While this was being done, I went to an office supply store on Ventura Boulevard to buy some greeting cards. There was a little basket at the cash register containing some pebbles in different colors, and they had little words on them. I reached in and pulled out a rose-pink one. And on the stone was written, *I am so happy that you are my sister.* My heart felt a shock, and I thought, *There's got to be ten of these in here.* So, much to the chagrin of the woman at the cash register, I upended the whole basket. And it was the only one with that saying. I went out to the car and just cried and cried. And I thought, *Is this a sign?* I don't know, but I have the pebble to this day.

"Two: On my fiftieth birthday, a friend went out to find me a present. She passed a toy store and saw a kind of magic wand with danglings on it and fluffy chiffon and sparkles. When she gave the gift to me, she said, 'A voice told me to go in and get you the magic wand. I didn't realize what was on the bottom of the wand until after I bought it.' So I unwrapped it, and on the bottom of the wand was a white ribbon with gold lettering on it that said, *Pamela.* So as far as I'm concerned, my sister came to wish me Happy Birthday when I turned fifty.

"That's inexplicable. I could be reading something into that, but so what? If it helps me to believe, there's nothing wrong with that."

"I often feel my sister is with me," says Sheilah, fifty-five, a softly pretty woman who leans forward and grows intense when she speaks about the impact on her of the death of her older sister, Beverly, of breast cancer, "a year and three months ago."

Seven years separated the two. "My sister was very maternal to me," says Sheilah, "and we were very, very close. Losing her was the worst thing that ever happened to me. But I do believe she is still with us. Visitations? My mom and I have them. Since my sister died, my mom—who can't smell anything—will get a strong sense of vanilla from time to time. A really strong smell. And she feels that my sister is there. Then about four months ago, my younger niece gave my mother a gift for her birthday of things scented with vanilla (completely coincidentally), and she said, 'Did you know that vanilla was my mother's favorite flavor?' We had no idea. So, yes, Beverly certainly is there with my mother.

"And at night, when I go to bed, I often feel that somebody's hand is right there [she touches the left side of her face in a caressing manner] and I know it's my sister. She would *never* abandon us. It wasn't a hallucination. It was her presence. It *is* her presence."

Sheilah goes on: "In Alice Sebold's book, *The Lovely Bones*, when the little girl dies she talks about being in her heaven and she tells what will take place in her heaven. Well, I always think of my sister's heaven. She's at Saks. She's playing tennis. She's getting a facial.... My sister told me once that when we got old we would be sitting on a porch and our rocking chairs would be together, toes touching. She painted a vivid picture. Two white chairs, a beautiful wide porch, and we would rock together and she would always take care of me. And I believed her."

"So you're not going to rock on the porch with your sister," I say.

"Yes, I am," Sheilah says with conviction. "I am, when I get to *my* heaven."

"For those who have a belief in an afterlife, there is a feeling of expectation that they'll be reunited with their loved one, and that itself is healing," says grief therapist Sherry Schachter. It *would* be nice to believe there is an afterlife, that the dead remain with us in more than memory. In fact, that is the quest undertaken by writer Justine Picardie. In a book called *If the Spirit Moves You*, she describes a yearlong odyssey to connect with the spirit of Ruth—her sister, only sibling, and best friend—who died of breast cancer at the age of thirty-three. Hoping to find a link, she visits psychics and spiritualists. Picardie's search leads her to the realization that if Ruth lives on, it is within herself... and the hope that someday she and her sister will meet again.

WHEN MY BROTHER CROSSED OVER...

In contrast, Robin Nolan does not question the inexplicable; she embraces it. "My brother, my beloved older brother, died—unexpectedly—when my first baby was eighteen days old," she wrote in an e-mail response to my request for people willing to share their stories of sibling loss. "I can tell you about the devastation. I can also tell you about the healing."

We speak several times.

The devastation: Robin was at home in San Jose, California, when she received a phone call from the coroner, who said, "I have some very sad news for you. Your brother has died." The facts were few: Mark, forty-one, had suffered a seizure, hit his head, and died. An autopsy was unable to determine the cause. "I felt stabbed in the heart," Robin says.

"The worst thing for me was that I had this incredible joy in my life—my new baby—and this incredible pain. There is a normal progression of life and death, but for the two to occur so closely, and out of the blue to lose a brother like that . . . It was like I fell into a hole, and nobody was available to get me out of it because everyone else was in their own hole. . . . My husband tried to comfort me. He said, 'Mark's probably in a better place,' which is not what I wanted to hear. That was the hardest part, I think, to accept that the death was so permanent."

A different scenario: Six years have gone by, and Robin speaks of that time as "when my brother crossed over." The choice of words reflects the wholly different view she now holds of life and death. "If you have any spirituality, any Christianity, anything, if you do believe in a higher power, you have to believe that the spirit of your loved one is with you," she says. "It just takes you a while to get to that point."

I ask her to explain the journey.

"If you think it's final, that death is when they put you in a box and there's nothing more, that is the hardest part of grief," she says. "If you think that you can't ever say the things that you wanted to say to your loved one, or give them a hug, that's the thing about loss that absolutely kills you from the inside out. But if you get to a point in your grieving when you start healing, then you can start believing that maybe there is a heaven and maybe the person is with you.

"I read a book, *Never Say Goodbye* by Patrick Mathews, who is a psychic medium. He explains that you don't have to say goodbye because your loved ones just crossed to the other side. To me it's like they step through a veil or they cross the river. You can't hug them or see them, but they're with you. I see Mark in my dreams. The most healing part is getting little signs and actually being able to believe that Mark is with me."

"Signs?" I ask.

"Whether it's the woodpecker outside my parents' window or it's finding pennies from heaven," she answers. "One day the car broke down and my dad got out and there were forty-five pennies on the ground, and it was two days before it would have been my brother's forty-fifth birthday. And then . . . I kept finding forty-seven cents: a quarter, four nickels and two pennies. I wondered why I was always finding forty-seven cents, and it was always shiny coins. Then I remembered that his girlfriend was forty-seven years old. So that was Mark. . . .

"And I'll tell you a story that let me know my brother was with us. We had a memorial service for Mark not too long ago and I invited all his friends. The next day, I had my son baptized, kind of to close one door and open another—a way of moving forward in our lives. My husband's aunt invited us for lunch, and her husband was cooking turkey burgers in the back yard. And my mom, dad, I, and my brother's daughter were wondering: How are we going to get out of this? We don't like turkey burgers. My husband's uncle was taking the burgers off the grill and he put them on a ceramic plate. The whole plate fell, burgers first, upside down, and the plate broke on top of the burgers. We all looked at one another and said, 'That was Mark,' because it was just so silly, and my brother was hilarious."

Robin sends me a copy of *Never Say Goodbye*, earmarking the chapter titled "Recognizing Their Communication." In it, the author directs readers: focus on how much is going on around you—background noises, leaves rustling—that you really never notice. Robin reads to me from the chapter. "The same holds true with noticing the connections of your loved ones in spirit. . . . The more you focus and notice, the more you will have from them. . . . "

At the very least (at least that's what I'm hearing), you may enjoy a very nice visit.

CHAPTER 12

The Rewards of Ritual

I regret that I did not speak at the funeral service for my sister. More to the point, I am sorry that I did not prepare a eulogy; whether I would actually have risen to speak the lines before the assembled mourners is incidental. It's the healing potential in the act itself—in thinking and writing about the one who has died—that I missed. But I did appreciate listening to others' recollections of Sybil as mother, grandmother, sibling, teacher, friend. Their memories, which they so generously shared, helped sustain me at a difficult time.

The impact of the funeral on the mourning process is remembered by others as well.

"I did the eulogy at Greg's funeral," says Sylvie, whose account of her brother's death was presented in the previous chapter. "We sat down as a family and threw out our thoughts, and I wrote them down. Being able to eulogize my brother was *very* helpful."

Because?

"Because I celebrated him, and he knows that. I talked through crying, but I also felt that this was a good thing. And in my heart I felt like he was saying Thank You."

Though they honor the dead, funerals are for the living. They help those who grieve face the reality of the passing. Death is certain. Mourning begins. For the survivors, the gathering of family and friends at a service also can provide emotional support at a time when it is sorely needed.

"The wake, the funeral were both very important," says Sylvie. "It took seven days for us to get my brother's body back to Illinois. It was heart-wrenching, unbelievable. Walking into the funeral home, seeing Greg's body laid out . . . I felt almost as if I was going to see my brother who wasn't there but who was there, if that makes any sense. I touched his chest. I touched his hair, which was soft and thick. That was helpful in a strange way. And I remember thinking, *This isn't Greg. Greg's essence is somewhere else now.* I grew up in the Episcopal Church, but I'm not a churchgoing person anymore. Still, the service was comforting.

"And then the wake began. I was astounded at the number of Greg's friends who showed up . . . people who'd attended high school with my brother, who no longer lived in Illinois. It was comforting. Then the most extraordinary thing happened. Some years before, I had a friend who had a friend whose brother died in a shocking and tragic accident. His favorite song was 'Let It Be.' My friend asked me if I could play that song on my guitar at his funeral when they brought the casket in, and I did that. . . . In the long line at the wake at Greg's funeral, a woman came up to me and introduced herself as the mother of the young man who had died. She had read about my brother's death in the paper, she said, and she just wanted to give me a hug. Her presence at my brother's funeral reminded me that you *can* survive. . . . So that was the wake. It was like a community coming together to celebrate the life of my precious brother."

Here's the chancy thing about funerals. When they are good, they can be very, very good—capturing the essence of the one who is lost, offering solace to those who grieve. But when they are bad, they can be horrid.

"I was not really present at my brother's funeral," I'm told by a good friend, Deanna. "There was so much going on, I was distracted. I was not present and that's the sadness and the loss and the overwhelming grief. My only explanation is that I put up a barrier, an emotional wall. And I didn't deal with it. First of all, we only saw this box. We didn't see the body. My sister and I felt the same: our brother Leonard was such a conniver, he probably faked his death. When he actually *was* buried, there was an outpouring of tears. At that moment in time, I felt that the loss was very real. Then we went back to the Elks Club—my brother was an Elk—and they were already celebrating his life, drinking and having a party. We left in a hurry."

When those who lead the ceremony pontificate, when they offer stock speeches on Life and Death, when the tone of the service is just plain wrong for the person being eulogized, we want to run screaming from the room. "The funeral for my brother was not helpful to me," said Heidi Horsley (Chapter 3). "I didn't like the choice of speakers or of music. Neither were representative of my brother."

At a professional meeting in a mid-Manhattan hotel, I meet Pam Vetter, forty-three, who lives in California. She tells me that she's a celebrant, explaining it as "someone who helps families create meaningful funeral services." I had never heard of a celebrant, but it seems to be a growing field of service. "It is not a profession I would have chosen," Pam says. "I wouldn't be in the funeral industry today if it were not for my sister's death and her funeral."

Pam's story: "I grew up in Pennsylvania's Amish country, the youngest of five children. My sister Diane was ten years older and we shared a bedroom. The idea was that if there were problems during the night the oldest could take care of the youngest. So we had a bond. We also had a bond over music. Diane owned the only stereo in the house. She had a collection of a few records—mostly Crosby Stills & Nash—that we would listen to over and over again. I wanted to grow up to be just like her. She became a high school teacher and went on to earn a doctorate in anthropology. Basically, she studied and accepted all people. She wanted to make whatever system she was involved in better. She was happily married and had a stepson. My sister was the one person I could always talk to in the world, the one who picked me up when I fell."

Suddenly, Diane was the one in need of help. At age forty-seven, she was diagnosed with endometrial cancer. "My sister knew she was dying," says Pam. "Everyone else's reaction was not to speak about the inevitable, but Diane *wanted* to talk about her death. She did everything she could. She researched her disease, including controversial trials, but ultimately had to face the reality that she would die. Her way of grieving was by working through it, and her bravery in going through the phases of her own mortality helped me also to accept her death.

"Diane planned her own funeral. She realized that we—the family, her husband, my parents—could not talk about the planning of her funeral," Pam says. "She made arrangements to videotape her final farewell words for her high school students because she didn't want them to get stuck in a place of grief. Instead, she wanted to give them a goal: find out what your mission is, and get it done. You have a limited time on this earth. You need to be productive. When the time of her death drew close, she called one of her former students who had become a mortician, met with him, chose her own casket, decided where she would be buried (in her husband's family plot). She had specific plans for the service. She wanted a Josh Groban song played.

"WHAT HURT was that those plans were not honored," Pam says. "Once Diane died, the pastor said NO to her requests, the service belonged to him. She had wanted my uncle (who is a pastor and had been visiting her) to preach, and our pastor said, 'No, he can't preach in my church.' We even had to negotiate to play the video. At the funeral, the pastor talked about Iraq and AIDS. He talked about nothing that had to do with my sister's life or death. He trivialized her life, and all he did was anger the family. Those moments got us stuck in our grieving."

There had to be a better way, Pam knew. Wanting to help others avoid the pain that she and her family experienced at Diane's funeral, she did some research and found an institute that trains celebrants ("It was the closest thing I could find to a eulogist," she says), took the required courses, and embarked on a career helping other families create meaningful funeral services. "The disposition of the body and the casket are one thing," Pam says. "The commemoration of life service is a completely different issue. Whether that comes as some sort of service in a church or in a funeral home or in words spoken and shared with a group of family and friends in a home, there has to be some official marker. I feel that with every family I help, every story that I share at a service, I am honoring my sister's life."

Rituals are important. They are an acknowledgment that we all have a need to think about those we have lost. Whether spiritual or secular, the funeral, the memorial service, the gathering of the clan for these events are useful in providing a constructive response to the question of *What do we do immediately following the death?*

But then there is the long goodbye—the days, weeks, years that follow a death. Some survivors continue to find guidance in religious practice. Jews who mourn their siblings may find comfort in reciting the traditional *kaddish* (mourner's prayer) in the synagogue for thirty days (*shloshim*), the prescribed period for when a sibling dies. (When it is a parent who has died, religious practice is for prayers to be said daily for eleven months.) On the anniversary of the death, Jewish families light *yahrzeit* (literally, a year's time) candles in the home and say *kaddish* in synagogue. Roman Catholics remember anniversaries by having Mass said in honor of the deceased. Protestants may place floral arrangements in the church.

CREATING RITUALS TO ADDRESS SPECIAL TIMES, MANAGE SPECIAL SADNESS

The memories and emotions rekindled through reminders of special times—birthday of the deceased, anniversary of the death, Christmas, Thanksgiving, and other notable times for the gathering of the clan—are called anniversary reactions. These reactions, which can begin before the event and last for days and weeks afterward, may cause survivors to experience sadness, loneliness, anger, anxiety, bad dreams—often at the same intensity as when the death occurred. Suddenly you are back there! One can expect that the holidays will cause a huge wave of emotion. Especially in the beginning, anniversary reactions require special attention and, often, special planning.

"There are religious rituals, but there also are informal rituals, ways that people devise to mark birthdays, anniversaries, or to otherwise provide comfort," says grief counselor Sherry Schachter. As an example, she tells of a man who lost his sister. "This was an older man, someone who had never married. Both parents were deceased. There was just him and his sister. The first Easter after the sister died, he was going to his niece's house. (He was very close with his sister's children.) He brought with him a very short, huge candle. He lit the candle at the table and the family said a little prayer. After dinner, he blew the candle out. Christmas time, when he went to his niece he brought the candle. Every holiday, he would bring this big fat candle and relight it and say a prayer or read a poem. He evoked his sister's memory. It was wonderful for his niece and her children as well."

Schachter then describes a ritual of her own devising. "My sister died two weeks before Passover," she says. "Everyone in the family would be coming to my house for the holiday—the first one we'd be celebrating without her—and I knew it would be difficult. I had read something in a popular magazine about kids writing on tablecloths, and I thought, *Oh, what a wonderful idea.* So I put down a tablecloth and some Sharpie permanent marker pens and I told my family that I wasn't setting the table until each of them wrote something. The first time they wrote something short: 'I'm thankful that we're together' or 'Thinking of past Passovers.' Whenever the family gathered thereafter, I would take out the cloth and people would start writing. Now they write 'I remember this . . .' Children too young to write can draw pictures. Over the years we have filled ten tablecloths. Many of the people who wrote are no longer here. These are tablecloths that are used. Yet it is a way to ritualize and memorialize . . . It's something any family can do.

"You know, everyone's thinking about the person who died—everyone's aware of their absence at the table, but no one's saying anything," she goes on. "If someone says 'Sis would have loved this' or 'I'm making her sweet potato recipe,' the person is remembered. And that's good."

A recipe, an anecdote, an empty chair at the table, a commemorative tablecloth—all are ways of looking backward that help one move forward.

MARKING THE MILESTONES

As unpredictable as grief is, we *can* reasonably predict that holidays, birthdays, and other special times will be difficult to deal with, especially when the loss of our sibling is recent. Many survivors report that the anticipation of the upcoming birthday or holiday is worse than the actual day. Grief counselors suggest that survivors tell important people in their life that this is a difficult time and let them know what they can do to help. One might say to a coworker, for example, "Friday is my late brother's birthday. I'd really like to have company for lunch on that day."

Some who grieve find a change of scenery helpful and plan a distraction such as a weekend away to help them get through the most difficult times. "After my sister died, I was not up to celebrating a family Christmas," says a surviving brother. "Her absence would have been too painful. I was not up to Christmas at all. Everyone was wishing a 'Merry this' and 'Happy that,' and it was not happy for me. So I went skiing in Colorado. I just needed to be away, doing something, keeping busy. The holidays passed and I was okay. That was five years ago, and I've since been able to rejoin the family celebrations. My brother will never be forgotten, but I have found that the intensity of the pain diminishes over time."

Another survivor finds peace in paying an annual birthday visit to her sister's grave, bringing a plant, reading a favorite poem. "It's our time together," she says. And a woman who was left "suddenly only" when her sister died four years ago tells me that the way she's devised to get through the holidays is by spending Thanksgiving and Christmas Day (formerly celebrated with her sister's family) as a volunteer in her church's soup kitchen. "It's a new tradition," she says, "one that keeps me busy and honors my sister's memory."

In my own experience, I have found it helpful to continue holiday traditions, to acknowledge that there's a vacant seat at the table, and to carry on. At Thanksgiving, when the whole family gets together, we've made it a custom to close the dinner service with a spirited (if off-key) rendition of "Over the river and through the woods . . . " expressly because Sybil had always requested that song. Her daughter plays the piano, her grandchildren join in. Sybil is with us still.

Other families deal with their grief by planning reunions around the anniversary of the death of the one who died. "Ours is a very complicated family—there are kids from different marriages and we live all over the country (including Alaska), yet we make it a point to get together on the anniversary of my brother Leonard's death," says Deanna. "It keeps us close as a family. As far as Leonard is concerned, we just feel that he's the closest to us at that time. If he's able to look down on us, I want him to see that the family is okay and to see that I'm watching out for them."

And still other survivors create new traditions or ways of honoring their loved ones. On the twentieth anniversary of her brother Michael's death, Marybeth Wahle threw a party. She created a video that featured photos of Michael from infancy on, cut to his favorite songs. "We had a Mass, then we had a party in celebration of his life," she says. "To mark what would have been his fiftieth birthday, I went through a folder of news clippings about him—he'd been a member of a memorable football team in our hometown. I collected all the accolades he won, put them together in a book, and had it copied for all of my siblings and for our children.

"Years after Michael's death, a number of students at his school set up a scholarship in his memory, and there is an award in my brother's name. While that is nice, what's most important is keeping him in our lives, having others remember and talk about him. That can mean the world to the person who has experienced the loss.

"It has for me."

CHAPTER 13

Continuing the Connection

It's a Saturday afternoon in August. My husband and I are heading off to a party being given by a friend to celebrate the milestone birthday of her husband. We've never been to their place, which is an hour's distance from our home. I read the directions to Noel, who is driving: "Left at the blinking traffic light, right at the red barn." Green fields stretch out on either side of us, the occasional small herd of cows providing a break in the landscape. Finally, we're close to our destination. We make our way up a long, narrow, winding road and reach a security gate. There is a buzzer, which we press, and we're admitted to the property. The gate closes behind us, and . . . nobody's there. No other cars, no people, no signs of life but for squirrels and songbirds.

"Take a look at the invitation," suggests Noel. I do as he says. The party's on *Sunday*. We've come a day early. Security guards arrive and, after I stammer out an explanation, they direct us back to the entrance (now an exit). Embarrassed and chagrined, I laugh hysterically all the way home. "Sybil would have loved this one," I say between gasps. My sister had a great appreciation of the absurd.

"Yes, she would have," Noel replies (though he is not laughing).

For a moment—a very precious moment—Sybil is with us in the car.

There are these moments, and incidents, when we find ourselves evoking the image of the deceased: "She would have loved this" . . . "He would have been so upset by that."

When they happen, GRAB THEM.

As we have seen (and contrary to past dogma), resolution of grief does not involve letting go of those we have lost but is helped by finding ways of holding on to them. Indeed, the word "resolution" is itself questionable, believes Phyllis Silverman, who has written on the importance of continuing bonds with the deceased. "I don't know what it means to *resolve* a death," she says. "I think people make *accommodations.* They find a way of living with their pain, with their angst."

Bereavement support includes finding ways to promote remembering. "It doesn't encourage you to live in the past but it encourages you to remember that the past is part of who you are today," says Silverman. "It's part of our feeling of attachment to people. We find comfortable places and we find ways of remembering."

Tangible objects help us to remember. Many survivors report that owning personal items that belonged to the deceased helps them maintain a feeling of connection. We are not talking here about something of great value (although items of value are not excluded). What's more important is that the physical item evokes a strong memory: in happier times, my brother played golf with these clubs; my sister made this necklace in a beading class.

Items of clothing can bring comfort. Hedda (Chapter 9) likes to sleep in an old shirt of her brother's. And Larry tells me that he's taken to wearing a beige cashmere cardigan with brown leather buttons that belonged to his kid brother, David, who was in his early fifties when he developed a fatal tumor. Not only were the brothers best friends, they also were business partners. "My brother had good taste," Larry says, explaining his acquisition of the sweater. He laughs self-consciously and then, in a voice I have to strain to hear, he adds, "When I wear David's sweater, I feel as if he still has his arm around my shoulders. A day doesn't go by without my thinking of him." In choosing to keep and wear the sweater, Larry acknowledges and makes sense of a part of his reality that has been transformed by his loss—that is, that his brother will never be wearing it again. He renegotiates his relationship with his brother but still manages to keep David close.

Poet Jeffrey Harrison wears his late brother's wedding band.

In a similar vein, I cherish a small brown ceramic vase that belonged to my sister. It has little monetary value, but I remember the day when, in one of our telephone visits, Sybil told me excitedly that she'd seen a vase she loved in a local shop. She described it in detail. "And," she said, "even though I don't need it, I went ahead and bought it." It was a rare act of self-indulgence. "Now I'm walking round and round the living room, wondering where to put it," she said, laughing.

I now have that vase, which serves as a reminder of an ordinary day in my sister's life that, by its acquisition, had become extraordinary.

"These so-called 'linking objects' help bereaved people hold on to their memories of the deceased, help confirm the reality of the life they lived, and help develop insight into the continuing impact those lives have on the living," write Gordon Riches, sociologist at the University of Derby, England, and Pam Dawson, bereavement services coordinator for the London borough of Bromley, in their book, *An Intimate Loneliness.*

But one doesn't need to inherit an object to feel linked to the sister or brother who has died. It's possible to create your own meaningful connection.

We remember with a picture. When I ask Sheilah if there's anything she does to keep the memory of her sister Beverly alive, she laughs and responds, "Do you want to see my apartment, the shrine? There are pictures of my sister *everywhere*. Pictures of the three of us—my mom, sister, and me—at different times in our lives. There are photographs of us on my desk at the office. So many things we did together, so many insignificant things that we did. I need to remember them all now."

Ada Thom Leonard experienced the death of her older brother Frank, of lung cancer, fifteen years ago. Speaking from her home in Florida, she says, "I'm standing here looking right at my kitchen god.... Actually, it's a picture of Frank, who was a great cook. I've got it placed right next to the stove, so that I feel like he's kind of watching me, putting in the garlic. I can't prepare anything without him overseeing me and making sure that I do it right.

"I do truly believe that there's a part of people that remains... that you never completely lose them," she says. "It helps me to keep my brother in my life, to think when I do something that he would have enjoyed—like cook a good meal or sign up for an African drumming class—*Frank would love this.*"

Writing helps get the message across. John Sherman's deeply affecting poem, "Sister" (page 5), was written in response to the death of his oldest sister Janice, who lost her battle with breast cancer at age fifty-two. What stands out for me most in speaking with John is not just his closeness with Janice but his love of the family unit. He describes a happy childhood: parents who were the envy of his friends, three close and caring sisters, their farmhouse on a hill that could be seen from a half mile away, letting him know that he was home. And that he was safe.

That sense of invulnerability followed him into adulthood. "Our family has been very fortunate in that we have lost very few people until they have become quite old," he says. "We used to joke that you had to shoot us—we just wouldn't die. That made it more of a shock, in a sense, when my sister died. Part of the untimeliness of losing a sibling was that our parents were then alive and well. I thought at the time of the obscenity of it, the obscenity of someone dying out of order."

Writing has helped John deal with the pain of his sister's death. He is convinced that writing can help others as well. "If you have something that you really need to think about and you can't share with anyone, it gets it out of your system to write about it," he says. "What you then do with it—keep it private, put it on the computer, or publish it—is your choice. But it is really very important to do that."

Writing, of course, is a way of telling the story. It explains the many memoirs in which survivors strive to eulogize the life of their brother or sister and to make sense of their death. It is, after all, the motivation behind this book and works by other writers who deal with sibling loss.

Survivors write articles about their deceased siblings in company newsletters, in magazines for the bereaved, in publications put out by organizations dealing with specific issues (such as loss by suicide or death caused in a driving accident). They share their stories on Web sites (see, for example, www.afsp.org, the Web site of the American Foundation for Suicide Prevention, or www.thegriefblog.com). They keep personal journals. They write about the deceased. They also pen unsent letters *to* the sister or brother who has died. It is their way of keeping the sibling alive in spirit. "Writing is a good way to deal with any unfinished business you may have with the deceased," says Dan Schaeffer, Ph.D., author of *How Do We Tell the Children?*, a guide to helping youngsters deal with loss. "Write what you need to say, take the paper to the cemetery, leave it at the grave."

We find special places in which to remember. A compelling reason for family and friends to visit such places as the Vietnam Veterans Memorial Wall in Washington, D.C., where they can see and touch the names of the deceased that have been etched on the memorial, make rubbings of the names, leave photos, flowers, and messages, or attend memorial services at Ground Zero, is the pull they feel to be at a place that connects them to the one who died.

Most of us, however, lose our loved ones in a less public manner yet still yearn for a place of commemoration. Many survivors speak of finding much-needed comfort and connection in visiting the cemetery on a regular basis, in tending the plot, in bringing flowers or other mementoes. (Others find it too painful to go.) "When my sister and I were kids, our family used to visit this place in Minnesota," says Michelle Linn-Gust, whose sister Denise died by suicide two weeks before her eighteenth birthday. "So I went there and took some pinecones and left them on her grave. I've also placed some sea shells there from places she hadn't been to." Going to the burial site, placing something on the grave is a way of maintaining connection.

We can also create a special place where we feel close to the one who died. Here is Jennie's story: "My big sister Lana struggled with Hodgkin's lymphoma in her twenties, was in remission for over a dozen years, and then had to face the illness again," she says. "This time, she didn't make it." Jennie became busy helping to care for Lana's son and daughter, who were teenagers at the time of their mother's death. "I went on automatic," she says of that first year. But then things calmed down. Lana's husband and children were able to work out a manageable routine, leaving the sister with time to reflect. "I'd heard about a program where, for a given sum donated to the Parks Department, you could have a plaque affixed to a park bench. I liked that idea. My sister loved the outdoors. I chose a bench adjacent to a dog exercise area (Lana also loved dogs). And now, when I want to visit with my sister, I take a walk to her bench, sit there, describe the day and the passersby (I like to think she sees them) and talk to her about whatever's on my mind. Sometimes, I just sit silently. But I've still had my time with Lana."

We create scrapbooks. I learn from Linda Pountney (see Chapter 7) about the value of scrapbooking in helping survivors remember and heal. You may recall that Linda's identical twin, Paula, died in a plane crash at the age of twenty-one. "Things that I couldn't cope with at that time pushed me into denying my grief and emotions," Linda says. More than a decade later, when her mother died, Linda was overwhelmed by feelings of grief. "I was with my mother when she died, so there was a sense of closure," she says. "I did not have that with my sister, who had been ripped away."

Needing now to confront that loss, Linda focused on Paula's life and on their relationship. She sifted through photographs of the two of them. "We were always together," she says. "Only three photos of our younger years existed where we were solo." She began to place the photos in a scrapbook, to give some shape to the memories. Paula's letters, testimonials of achievement, even a lock of her hair were included. "Every day brought new healing as I created a gigantic scrapbook album," Linda says.

She created new rituals. "One day, on our mutual birthday, I went with a friend to the cemetery and we ate sundaes at the grave site to honor Paula's love of them. We took photos and I added them to the album. It's an especially helpful way to deal with anniversary reactions." Linda and her husband are now in the business of manufacturing fabric-covered scrapbook albums. "The act of working with the memories and creating something of beauty became a very positive bereavement ritual for me," she says. "Not only has scrapbooking helped me look back, it helps the relationship with my sister to continue."

We create memorials. Survivors set up Web pages to honor their siblings' memory. Some create or contribute to quilts, like the second national Faces of Suicide Sibling Quilt (for more information, see the Suicide Prevention Action Network, www.spanusa.org). Others find outlets in different kinds of creative endeavor. "My brother George was involved in woodworking," I'm told by Karen, a sister who was left "only" by his death. "I'd never held a hammer or saw in my hand, but after he died I took a course in woodworking at the local Y. It was a way, I felt, to get closer to him. My first project was a simple table—something that a child might make in shop class. I have that table in my home. When I look at it, as I do every day, I think of George. I've since moved on to more complex projects, and I love it. Everything I make, I feel that George is working with me."

We remember by doing good works. The brother who organizes blood drives in memory of his sibling who died of a rare blood disease . . . the surviving sister who addresses school groups on the danger of drugs after her brother died of an overdose . . . the family that sets up a scholarship or establishes an event, asking that donations be made to a designated charity or cause . . . Such stories of turning tragic events into positive behaviors are many.

We pay tribute to those who have died when we make their cares genuinely our own. In a sense, then, they live on through the good that we do. You will recall, for example, that Erin St. John Kelly and her family continued the humanitarian work of her brother James when they set up a foundation to enable the education of children raised in orphanages in India. By honoring James's passion for helping others, the survivors find that they also have helped themselves. Similarly, the Siller family's involvement in the Tunnel to Towers Run and the work of the foundation established in their brother Stephen's memory not only benefits disadvantaged children but serves the need of Stephen's surviving siblings to heal. "There was no way we were going to let Steve go," says his brother, Russell.

But it isn't necessary to create a run or set up a tournament. Many survivors join an established event (a marathon, a walk to promote breast cancer awareness), raising funds in memory of their deceased sibling. We remember by having an activity to honor the memory of the one who has died.

The continuing bond with the deceased may also influence a survivor's choice of career. In doing research for this book, I find several people who entered the helping professions seeking to make sense of the loss of their sibling and wound up dedicating themselves to working with others who struggle with similar demons. "Were it not for my brother's [or sister's] death, I would not be doing this," I hear from one or another writer or grief professional. I feel grateful that they have chosen this way to continue the connection . . . that they help guide us in ways to remember the past as we lead our lives in the present and perhaps get a glimpse of the future.

The same week that my sister Sybil died, my grandson Charlie was born.

I wish they could have known each other.

CHAPTER 14

How *Do* We Help Someone Who Is Grieving?

An invitation to attend the wedding of the son of good friends arrived in the mail. We were very fond of the groom, a bright and generous young man, and had met his intended, whom we deemed worthy of him—no small praise. My husband and I accepted with pleasure, made our travel plans to the city where the event was to take place, reserved a room at the designated hotel, and looked forward to celebrating with family and friends. Then my sister died. In the weeks that followed, the wedding became the furthest thing from my mind. Still, the invitation remained tacked up on my bulletin board, and I had to decide whether to change our acceptance to regrets. *Life goes on*, I reasoned, and we went to the wedding.

It was the wrong decision. Though I managed to get through the ceremony (my tears could have been chalked up to sentimentality), the reception that followed was a different matter entirely. While those around me celebrated the new couple, I experienced the crush of people, clinking of glasses, passing of hors d'oeuvres, volume and beat of the band as an assault.

"I cannot manage this right now," I said softly to Noel.

What helped is that he quickly and calmly brought me back to the hotel. What helped is that he did not question my decision, did not try to talk me into staying longer—perhaps to wait until we'd had something to eat. What helped is that he understood. I no longer felt alone.

In speaking with other survivors of sibling loss, I have time and again been impressed by their accounts of people who behaved in ways that the mourners found helpful (sometimes as small a gesture as a friend who just sat by and held their hand is long remembered as a great kindness) while other people said and did things that added to their grief. There are lessons in these stories.

"Bereavement concerns all of us," says Phyllis Silverman, a noted researcher in the field. "The thing that really concerns me is that we're medicalizing grief—we're making it into an emotional problem for which we need psychiatric help. I think that's not a good idea. People have to learn to live through the pain. And unfortunately, if the one who's bereaved has lost a sibling, this may be the first death that the friends of the survivor have met, and they haven't any experience in dealing with grief. So how *do* we prepare? How do we help our friends and each other?"

That is what we look at here.

BE PRESENT

When her brother, Ned, died in a car accident at the age of twenty-one, Pam Teibel, then eighteen, was devastated (see Chapter 10). Almost immediately, the house was filled with people. There was a wake. "But my best friend, who meant well but wasn't Catholic, didn't know about wakes, didn't understand the process by which people gather to support the family, and so she communicated to my friends to just stay away until the funeral," Pam says. "I was left alone. That was incredibly difficult for me."

"Do not assume that a friend wants to mourn alone," writes Sol Gordon, professor emeritus of child and family studies at Syracuse University, in his book, *Is There Anything I Can Do? Helping a Friend When Times Are Tough*. "Few mourners want privacy for very long. Most want and need contact."

Embrace your friend physically and emotionally.

If you do not know what to say, a simple "I'm sorry" will suffice. Especially in the initial period following the death, the mourner may be struggling to sort out her feelings, and the knowledge that she is not alone may be all that is needed.

Karen Snepp, the bereaved sibling who served as president of the board of The Compassionate Friends, speaks to this point. "There's still a lot of discomfort and stigma around the subject of death," she says. "After my brother, Dave, died of cancer, one of the biggest challenges for me was feeling that I had to rescue others around me, to put *them* at ease. At a time when you're most vulnerable, you have to be the teacher. That was exhausting. We need to give survivors permission to talk about the life *and* death of the one they lost. Don't deny that it happened. Even if you just say 'I'm sorry,' then that takes the elephant out of the room." She adds, "If you have a story about the person who died, share it. It's kind of cool to learn new things about the person after they're gone."

IF YOU CANNOT BE PRESENT, PLACE A PHONE CALL

If the mourner doesn't come to the phone, understand that this might be a difficult moment. Don't take umbrage or feel that you've discharged your obligation. Wait a while and call again.

WRITE A LETTER

"What helped me after my sister, Beverly, died is when people wrote to me, sharing a memory of her," says Sheilah (see Chapter 11). "I knew she had a lot of friends, but I hadn't realized the many different ways in which she'd touched people's lives and that they, too, now felt a void caused by Beverly's passing. The most comforting letters I received came from people of faith. They said all the right things. They weren't afraid to write about feelings and hope. I saved those letters, and I take them out and read them when I'm feeling especially lonely without my sister. It's like we're having a visit, and that lifts my spirits."

BE A GOOD LISTENER

"It is hard to know what to say to a person who has been struck by tragedy, but it is easier to know what not to say," writes Rabbi Harold Kushner in *When Bad Things Happen to Good People*, a modern classic that has brought solace and hope to many. "Anything critical of the mourner ('Don't take it so hard,' 'Try to hold back your tears, you're upsetting people') is wrong. Anything which tries to minimize the mourner's pain ('It's probably for the best,' 'It could be a lot worse,' 'She's better off now') is likely to be misguided and unappreciated."

In the book, Kushner recounts the biblical story of Job, who, after suffering one tragic event after another, ends up being criticized by the three friends who ostensibly came to console him. He writes, "[Job] needed friends who would permit him to be angry, to cry and to scream, much more than he needed friends who would urge him to be an example of patience and piety to others. He needed people to say, 'Yes, what happened to you is terrible and makes no sense,' not people who would say, 'Cheer up, Job, it's not all that bad.' And that was where his friends let him down."

Job's friends did at least two things right, says the rabbi. First of all, they came. "And secondly," he writes, "they listened. According to the biblical account, they sat with Job for several days, not saying anything, while Job poured out his grief and anger. That, I suspect, was the most helpful part of their visit."

Like Job, those who mourn the death of a sibling are likely to feel grief and anger. They are likely to feel guilt. They are likely to feel that what happened is terrible and makes no sense. At a time of great pain, we know, there is solace in telling their story. We help those who grieve by encouraging them to share their memories with us and by listening to what they have to say.

RESIST THE IMPULSE TO TRADE STORIES

What frequently happens during condolence visits, however, is quite the opposite. "People come and tell you their own stories," says Norma, forty-three, who recently marked the first anniversary of her sister Katie's death, from breast cancer, at the age of forty-five. "So many people had cancer stories to share, and they did . . . in great detail. But I didn't want to hear about their loved ones. This was *Katie* I was mourning. This wasn't just the latest victim of a plague."

I find myself nodding. I remember, when my father died of bladder cancer some forty years ago, sitting *shiva* with my mother, brother, and sister at my parents' home. Each day, visitors would stream into the house, directing their attention to one or another of us mourners. And every evening, after the last caller had gone, we would turn to one another and ask, "What's the most tragic story that you heard about today?"

People do this because they are uncomfortable talking about the one who has just died—the wound is still too fresh. They do this in an attempt to distract the newly bereaved from the present pain. They tell *their* stories to show they understand: I, too, have been in pain.

Statements such as "I know how you feel" and "I know what you're going through" are not helpful. Every life is different, each loss unique.

"This is not about *your* pain," Sol Gordon says. "Listen."

"The way to make bereaved people feel better is to ask them about the person who has died," suggests Phyllis Silverman. "Ask them about their relationship to that person. Ask: What's it like for you now? Don't give advice. Don't try to make people feel better. Take your cues from them. If they're really distraught and upset, and if they sometimes want to go out for a walk, take them out for a walk. If they enjoy a cup of coffee, go out and have some coffee. But don't think you have to make them feel better in a way that is artificial. Just be there and hear them. Don't think you have to say something profound to make the pain go away."

PROVIDE CONCRETE ASSISTANCE

Please don't say to someone struggling with a recent loss, "Let me know if there's anything I can do." Chances are the bereaved person will not be able to focus on a specific need or may feel uncomfortable asking for assistance. We help someone who's grieving when we anticipate their needs and take actions to meet them. Following the death of her brother, for example, Marybeth Wahle felt greatly supported when a college roommate understood that the devastated sister was torn between a need to be in school and a desire to be at home with her grieving family. The roommate handed over the keys to her car and said, "You can have this if ever you feel the need to go home or I will drive you there."

People caught up in grief often neglect some of the activities of daily living. We help them when we take over some of the chores. Going to the grocery store, bringing over prepared food, offering to pick up someone's mail from the post office or their child from school, perhaps raking their leaves or shoveling their walk during the difficult days can make a difference, not just in managing the chores but in affirming, for the survivor, the fact that he or she is not alone but is part of a caring community.

STAY IN TOUCH

The funeral's over, the official mourning period has ended, and those friends and family members who came together in sorrow now disperse to points distant. This is the time when a call or visit will be welcome, an invitation to the bereaved to join you for a cup of coffee, a dinner out or a walk on the beach may be just the thing.

Be patient with those who are grieving and allow them the time they need to heal.

CHAPTER 15

What About Me?

LIFE IS A FRAGILE THING

The incalculable loss of a brother or sister makes painfully clear to us that life is short and death is random. "When you're younger, there's a kind of fearlessness, a live-forever feeling," says a woman in her forties, looking back at the death of her kid brother five years earlier. "You lose your grandparents, you may even lose your parents.... That's to be expected, though the timing and manner of their death can still be distressing. But when your sibling dies, it is too close to home. And you think, *Yes, that could be me. It could happen to me.*"

We think about our own mortality. "Don't be embarrassed if one of the thoughts that goes through your mind after the loss of a sibling is *Am I next?*" writes psychologist P. Gill White, whose career was shaped by the early loss of her sister. "Our siblings are our peers, so it makes sense that we think in this way at times."

Michelle Linn-Gust, whose sister, Denise, died by suicide at age seventeen, goes further. "My sister's death really gave me a sense of my own mortality," she says. "We're not promised anything, and I learned that early, and I fear (even though it's probably irrational) that I'm going to lose my own life in some way today or tomorrow."

We pay attention to the quality of our lives. This strong awareness that life is finite has a positive side in spurring surviving siblings to live their days fully—to live, in a sense, for two. "I was always an overachiever, but I'm probably *more* of an overachiever because of my sister's death," says Linn-Gust. "Denise didn't get to do all the things that she wanted with her life, so I'm trying to do even more with mine."

Marian Sandmaier similarly feels a responsibility to make the most of her life. "My brother Bob was cut down at age thirty-three, and I'm still here," she says. "So when it comes to things I want in life, I think '*Go for it.*' He would want me to. Bob was the essence of 'alive.' His eyes were always gleaming. He was often smiling. He was always in motion. His death has taught me an important lesson: to make the most of my life."

We reinforce other of our relationships. Following the death of a sister or brother, many surviving siblings consciously strengthen their relationships with remaining siblings, or with spouses, partners, close friends. "Losing someone you love, especially when it happens with little or no warning, teaches you to treasure the people in your life," says Alison, whose "healthy" sister fell dead of a heart attack at the age of forty-three. "It teaches you to remember to say I love you, to say the things you need to say and not put things off."

We reinvent ourselves. "We can never be the person we were to the one who has died," says Heather Summerhayes Cariou, whose sister Pam succumbed to cystic fibrosis. "I can never be the Heather I was to Pam except in memory. We are who we are to different people. And when the person is gone, there's a change of identity. You have to figure out: Who am I without my brother or sister in my life? Before my sister's death, the essential question in my life was 'What do I want to be?' After Pam died, it became 'What kind of person do I want to be? Do I want to be a bitter person or do I want to be a forgiving person?' I want Pam to know me as I am now, to know who I am becoming. I want my me to be a constant gift to her, to the memory of her."

We move on but not away. The fortunate among us eventually find serenity. Following the death of his brother, Eugene, of pneumonia at age forty-two, Hollis railed against God, man, and the medical establishment. In more ways than one, as he saw it, life wasn't fair. "I'd been through a lot of professional turmoil in the years leading up to my brother's death," he says. "I got caught up in the dot.com boom, had a high-profile job, and lost all that. I thought it was the end of the world. . . .

"Since Eugene died, my anxiety about such things has diminished," he goes on. "While I continue to go through professional upheavals, those types of things seem very trivial to me now. Quite honestly, things that I might have found devastating prior to my brother's death have barely fazed me following his death. I learned the hard way about what's really important and gained a greater level of serenity, if you will.

"My ongoing regret is that I'm unable to share this with my brother."

And we remember. We honor the sisters and brothers we have lost by remembering their lives.

We honor them by letting others in our lives know that we value them and their friendship.

We honor them by living well: fulfilling the promise of our gifts; being compassionate and caring; appreciating what we have even as we are mindful of what we have lost.

Postscript

I once wrote a book called *A Hole in My Heart*, about the long-term effects of divorce on its children. The dedication page read:

For Sybil

In Gratitude and Love

So it is with some surprise that I hear a young woman use this same phrase in speaking to me about the death of her sibling. "It really is a hole in your heart that never goes away," she says, "but you move on. Anybody who has ever lost somebody close to them knows that, somehow, you get this inner strength to cope. You don't know how you do it, but nature sort of helps you. It doesn't mean that the loss isn't significant, because it is significant. It changes your life."

Yes it does.

Resources

ORGANIZATIONS/WEB SITES

Healing the Grieving Heart
www.thegriefblog.com

Interactive forum created by Drs. Gloria and Heidi Horsley provides education, stories, referral to Compassionate Friends chapter locations and Web sites.

The Sibling Connection
www.counselingstlouis.net

A resource for anyone who has lost a sister or brother, created and maintained by St. Louis-based therapist P. Gill White, author of *Sibling Grief.* Contains extensive bibliography, articles, message board.

Bereaved Parents of the USA
www.bereavedparentsusa.org
National office: P.O. Box 95
Park Forest, IL 60466
(708) 748-7866

National nonprofit self-help group that offers support, understanding, compassion, and hope to the newly bereaved—parents, grandparents, siblings. Chapters hold support meetings. Helpful articles, resource links on Web site.

The Compassionate Friends
www.compassionatefriends.org
P.O. Box 3696
Oak Brook, IL 60522-0010
Toll-Free (877) 969-0010

National organization offering friendship and support to bereaved parents, siblings, and grandparents. Online resources as well as a listing of chapters in each state. National newsletter. Also offers an online support community that does not offer grief counseling. It exists for grief support—a safe place to share feelings and grief experiences. Sibling support rooms are for bereaved siblings eighteen years of age and older.

Twinless Twins
www.twinlesstwins.org
P.O. Box 980481
Ypsilanti, MI 48198-0481
(888) 205-8962

Provides support for twins and other multiples who have lost their twin due to death or estrangement at any age. National conference, regional groups.

Association for Death Education and Counseling/
The Thanatology Association
www.adec.org

Maintains a list of grief counselors. Provides information on coping with loss.

Active Minds
www.activemindsoncampus.org
2647 Connecticut Avenue, NW
Suite 200
Washington, D.C. 20008
(202) 332-9595

Peer-to-peer organization with chapters at over 100 college campuses, dedicated to raising awareness of mental health issues, offering support, education, advocacy.

American Association of Suicidology
www.suicidology.org
5221 Wisconsin Avenue, NW
Washington, D.C. 20015
(202) 237-2280

Education and resource organization dedicated to the understanding and prevention of suicide. List of support groups nationwide, survivor stories. Helpful information.

American Foundation for Suicide Prevention
www.afsp.org
120 Wall Street
22nd floor
New York, NY 10005

Survivor stories available on Web site. Has a helpful resource, *Coping with Suicide Loss.*

Suicide Prevention Action Network USA (SPAN)
www.spanusa.org
1025 Vermont Avenue, NW
Suite 1066
Washington, D.C. 20005

Suicide prevention and survivor resources. Goal: to create a way for those who have lost someone to suicide to transform their grief into positive action to prevent further tragedies.

National Suicide Hotline

(800) 784-2433

Will direct you to a program nearest to you.

Bibliography

Ascher, Barbara Lazear. *Landscape without Gravity: A Memoir of Grief.* New York: Penguin Books, 1994.

Attig, Thomas. *How We Grieve: Relearning the World.* Oxford: Oxford University Press, 1996.

Bank, Stephen P., and Michael D. Kahn. *The Sibling Bond.* New York: Basic Books, 1982, 1997.

Becvar, Dorothy S. *In the Presence of Grief.* New York: The Guilford Press, 2001.

Boss, Pauline. *Ambiguous Loss: Learning to Live with Unresolved Grief.* Cambridge: Harvard University Press, 2000.

Cariou, Heather Summerhayes. *Sixtyfive Roses: A Sister's Memoir.* Toronto, Canada: McArthur & Company, 2006.

Cicirelli, Victor G. *Sibling Relationships across the Life Span.* New York: Plenum Press, 1995.

Colgrove, Melba, Harold H. Bloomfield, and Peter McWilliams. *How to Survive the Loss of a Love.* Los Angeles: Prelude Press, last revision 1996.

Conway, Jill Ker. *The Road from Coorain.* New York: Vintage Books, 1989.

DeVita-Raeburn, Elizabeth. *The Empty Room.* New York: Scribner, 2004.

Doka, Kenneth J., and Joyce D. Davidson. *Living with Grief: Who We Are, How We Grieve.* Philadelphia: Bruner/Mazel, 1986.

Donnelly, Katherine Fair. *Recovering from the Loss of a Sibling.* New York: Dodd, Mead & Company, 1988.

Fanos, Joanna H. *Sibling Loss.* Mahwah, NJ: Lawrence Erlbaum Associates, 1996.

Gordon, Sol. *"Is There Anything I Can Do?": Helping a Friend When Times Are Tough.* New York: Delacorte Press, 1994.

Grollman, Earl A. *Living with Loss, Healing with Hope: A Jewish Perspective.* Boston: Beacon Press, 2000.

Grollman, Earl A., and Max Malikow. *Living When a Young Friend Commits Suicide.* Boston: Beacon Press, 1999.

Hundley, Mark E. *Awaken to Good Mourning.* Plano, TX: Awaken Publications, 1993.

Kincaid, Jamaica. *My Brother*. New York: Farrar, Straus & Giroux, 1997.

Klass, Dennis, Phyllis R. Silverman, and Steven L. Nickman. *Continuing Bonds: New Understandings of Grief*. Washington, D.C.: Taylor & Francis, 1996.

Kushner, Harold S. *When Bad Things Happen to Good People*. New York: Schocken Books, 1981.

LaGrand, Louis E. *Messages and Miracles: Extraordinary Experiences of the Bereaved*. St. Paul: Llewellyn Publications, 1999.

Levine, Stephen. *Who Dies?* New York: Anchor Books, 1982.

Linn-Gust, Michelle. *Do They Have Bad Days in Heaven? Surviving the Suicide Loss of a Sibling*. Atlanta: Bolton Press, 2001.

Martel, Yann. *Life of Pi*. New York: Penguin, 2001.

Mathews, Patrick. *Never Say Goodbye*. St. Paul: Llewellyn Publications, 2003.

Mead, Margaret. *Blackberry Winter*. New York: Kodansha International, 1995.

Neimeyer, Robert A. *Lessons of Loss: A Guide to Coping*. Memphis: Center for the Study of Loss and Transition, 2000.

Picardie, Justine. *If the Spirit Moves You: Life and Love after Death*. New York: Riverhead Books, 2002.

Rando, Therese A. *How to Go On Living When Someone You Love Dies*. New York: Bantam Books, 1991.

Riches, Gordon, and Pam Dawson. *An Intimate Loneliness: Supporting Bereaved Parents and Siblings*. Buckingham, England: Open University Press, 2000.

Rosen, Helen. *Unspoken Grief: Coping with Childhood Sibling Loss*. Lexington: Lexington Books, 1986.

Sandmaier, Marian. *Original Kin: The Search for Connection among Adult Sisters and Brothers*. New York: Plume, 1995.

Segal, Nancy L. *Entwined Lives: Twins and What They Tell Us about Human Behavior*. New York: Plume, 2000.

Segal, Nancy L. *Indivisible by Two: Lives of Extraordinary Twins*. Cambridge: Harvard University Press, 2005.

Smolin, Ann, and John Guinan. *Healing after the Suicide of a Loved One*. New York: Fireside, 1993.

Terkel, Studs. *Will the Circle Be Unbroken: Reflections on Death, Rebirth and Hunger for a Faith*. New York: The New Press, 2001.

Viorst, Judith. *Necessary Losses*. New York: Simon & Schuster, 1986.

Welshons, John E. *Awakening from Grief*. Little Falls, NJ: Open Heart Publications, 2000.

White, P. Gill. *Sibling Grief: Healing after the Death of a Sister or Brother*. Lincoln: iUniverse, 2006.

Wray, T. J. *Surviving the Death of a Sibling*. New York: Three Rivers Press, 2003.

Index

Acknowledgments

This book was written with the assistance and encouragement of many people. Foremost among them are the men and women who so generously shared their experiences and emotions with me. Losing a sister or brother is not an easy subject to talk about, yet in interview after interview I found both caring and candor. I am very grateful.

To the many professionals who shared their knowledge and their thoughts with me (and now with my readers) goes my appreciation.

MariAn Gail Brown, a special woman, merits special mention. A friend and talented journalist, she not only validated my belief that the subject of sibling loss deserved greater attention, but she put me in touch with Debora Carvalko, able editor at Praeger, who agreed. Thanks, also, to my agent Jim Levine for his general support of my work.

Writers do not work in a vacuum. I am fortunate to have the support of a loving family—sons, daughters-in-law, extraordinary grandchildren—but must single out two of its members for special commendation. Orin Berman, knowledgeable and patient, could always be called upon to deal with technical crises. Noel Berman is there for me, always, in every other way.

About the Author

CLAIRE BERMAN is a freelance writer, former director of public education for the Child Welfare League of America, and former Executive Council member for the American Society of Journalists and Authors. Specializing in writing about the emotional dimensions of family relationships, she has authored or coauthored eight books, and her articles have appeared in publications including *Reader's Digest*, *McCall's*, *Family Circle*, *Good Housekeeping*, *Woman's Day*, and *The New York Times Magazine*. Berman has appeared on the *Today* show and has been featured in *People* magazine.